EMMAU

the way of faith

STAGE 3: GROWTH

EMMAUS

the way of faith

STAGE 3: GROWTH

Knowing God

Four short courses for growing Christians

Stephen Cottrell, Steven Croft,
John Finney, Felicity Lawson and Robert Warren

CHURCH HOUSE
PUBLISHING

Church House Publishing
Church House
Great Smith Street
London
SW1P 3NZ
Tel: 020 7898 1451
Fax: 020 7898 1449

ISBN 0 7151 4032 9

Second edition published 2005 by Church House Publishing

First published 1996 by The National Society/Church House Publishing
and The Bible Society.

CD-ROM created by Ambit New Media
www.ambitnewmedia.com

Cover design by Church House Publishing

Cover photograph © Marcus Perkins 2003

Printed in England by Biddles Ltd, King's Lynn

Contents

CD-ROM contents

* Indicates material not in main text of book and supplied separately.

■ *members' handouts and supplementary handouts as PDF files;*

■ *twelve handouts used for introducing the idea of* Emmaus *to churches;**

■ *five PowerPoint presentations (which can also be adapted into OHP slides) for introducing the idea of* Emmaus *to churches;**

■ Emmaus *posters;**

■ Emmaus *Resources Catalogue;*

■ *links to the* Emmaus *web site;*

■ *help page.*

Acknowledgements

Every effort has been made to trace and contact copyright holders. If there are any inadvertent omissions we apologise to those concerned.

Extracts from the following are reproduced by permission:

The Scripture quotations contained herein are from *The New Revised Standard Version of the Bible*, copyright © 1989 by the Division of Christian Education of the National Council of the Churches of Christ in the USA. All rights reserved.

Common Worship: Services and Prayers for the Church of England (2000) is copyright © The Archbishops' Council.

John Blanchard, *Will the Real Jesus Please Stand Up*, Evangelical Press, 1989. Used by permission of the publisher.

Steven Croft, *Growing New Christians*, CPAS/Marshall Pickering, an imprint of HarperCollins Publishers Limited, 1993.

Brian Doerksen, 'Refiner's fire'. Copyright © 1990 Mercy/Vineyard Publishing, Administered in the UK and Eire by Integrity's Hosanna! Music, PO Box 101, Eastbourne, East Sussex BN21 4SZ. All rights reserved. International copyright secured. Used by permission.

Bill and Lynne Hybels, *Rediscovering Church*, Copyright © 1995 by Bill Hybels. Used by permission of Zondervan Publishing House.

Daniel Iverson, 'Spirit of the living God'. Copyright © 1963 Birdwing Music/Alliance Media Ltd. Administered by CopyCare, PO Box 77, Hailsham BN27 3EF. Used by permission.

C. S. Lewis, *Mere Christianity*, Collins Fontana Books, 1952. Reproduced by permission of HarperCollins Publishers Ltd.

Peter Marshall, *Mr Jones, Meet the Master*, Peter Davies Ltd (William Heinemann), 1954. Reprinted by permission of Reed Consumer Books.

The Mystery of Salvation (1995), copyright © The Central Board of Finance of the Church of England.

William Temple, *Readings in St John's Gospel*, Macmillan, 1947.

John Watson, 'Living water'. Copyright © 1986 Ampelos Music. Administered by CopyCare, PO Box 77, Hailsham, BN27 3EF. Used by permission.

Extracts from T. S. Eliot, *Choruses from 'The Rock', Collected Poems 1909–1962*, Faber & Faber Ltd.

Extracts from Robert Warren, *An Affair of the Heart,* Highland, 1994.

Extracts from *A Wee Worship Book*, Wild Goose Worship Group, 1989, copyright © 1989 WGRG, Iona Community, Pearce Institute, 840 Govan Road, Glasgow, G51 3UU, Scotland.

Introducing the *Emmaus* Growth materials

What are the Growth materials?

The *Emmaus* Growth courses are published in three books (see diagram below). Each book contains four or five short modules on aspects of Christian living.

What is the purpose of the Growth materials?

The *Emmaus* Growth materials are intended to offer Christians an opportunity to deepen their understanding of Christian living and discipleship. They may be used as follow-on from a nurture course – whether you've already used *Emmaus* or not.

The materials may be used with new Christians, to enable them to lay firm foundations, and to help more mature Christians take a fresh look at familiar topics.

What's in each of the Growth books?

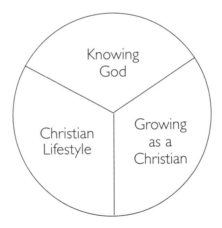

Knowing God

1 Living the gospel (4 sessions)

A simple course on sharing our faith with others who make up our own network of relationships.

2 Knowing the Father (4 sessions)

Our experience of God leading to an appreciation of God as Holy Trinity.

3 Knowing Jesus (4 sessions)

The person of Jesus and a relationship with him as Lord.

4 Come, Holy Spirit (4 sessions)

The work of the Holy Spirit in the life of individual Christians, in the Church and in the world.

Growing as a Christian

 1 Growing in prayer (4 sessions)

Different methods and understandings of prayer, including practical help and encouragement. The course is based around the Lord's Prayer.

 2 Growing in the Scriptures (5 sessions)

The nature and the meaning of the scriptures and practical help in understanding and reading the Bible.

 3 Being church (4 sessions)

What does it mean to belong? Different models and understandings of the Church.

 4 Growing in worship – understanding the sacraments (5 sessions)

An exploration of Christian worship as an unfolding celebration of the Easter mystery and of the sacraments as communion with the risen Lord.

 5 Life, death and Christian hope (3 sessions)

An exploration of the Christian hope, the last things and the Christian attitude to death.

Christian Lifestyle

 1 Living images (4 sessions)

There is a search for meaning in life in today's society and a longing to live life to the full. But what does it mean to do that? How can we be fully human?

 2 Overcoming evil (5 sessions)

As soon as we seek to be fully human we discover problems. People are not perfect and life is not fair. There is a flaw in the whole of creation. The reality, which the Christian tradition calls sin, is understood as being like gravity. How do we understand and address this aspect of life?

3   **Personal identity** (5 sessions)

How do we understand ourselves so we can love others? This session explores how that true self can be rightly affirmed, nourished and expressed in life.

4   **Called into life** (4 sessions)

This course is intended to help every baptized believer know more about what it means to have a vocation – not just for the work we do, if we are employed, but for who we are and how we live our lives before God.

How do I use the Growth materials?

Each Growth book has four or five modules. Within each module there are three, four or five sessions.

Of course, you can be as flexible as you wish with the material. You do not have to use each of the sessions and you can cover material in whatever order and over whatever period of time suits the needs of your group.

You may choose to use some of the sessions or modules with an enquirers' group. Some groups have found the 'Personal identity' module from Christian Lifestyle particularly appropriate.

Leading a Growth course

The materials have been designed so that courses can be led by lay people or clergy, but in most churches lay-led groups will be better. Experience does help, but the material here has been used successfully by people who have never led groups before.

There is some teaching input to be delivered in each session, but this comes in manageable chunks with detailed and straightforward notes. The main emphasis is not on the leader talking to the group, but on facilitating sharing, reflection, Bible study and discussion.

Your group may already have explored the basics of Christian faith in the *Emmaus* Nurture course or in some other way. Or you may be an established house group looking for a new direction. Or perhaps a group of Christians coming together for the first time in your church to go deeper in faith.

Whichever kind of group you will be leading, the leader's main task in all these courses will be to encourage and enable exploration and discussion. Growth in the Christian life is not just about accumulating knowledge. There are things to learn, but growth is about initiation into a way of life, rather than just gaining possession of a body of information.

In engaging with this material, group members will be encouraged to think deeply about their own experience of life and so enter into dialogue with the Christian tradition. In this way people will make the tradition their own. Faith will not be second-hand knowledge but first-hand experience. This understanding is central to everything that happens on the Way of Faith.

No two groups are the same, so it is important for each group leader to feel free to adapt the material to suit the particular needs and gifts of individuals within each particular group. Don't feel you need to tackle all the courses in one book, or do them in the order given. Take them one at a time. Then, towards the end of each course, if your group is staying together, think and pray and talk together about whether to tackle another – or use some different material.

Preparation

A separate booklet, *Leading an Emmaus Group*, contains helpful advice on leading and running any kind of nurture or growth group.

In your preparation for each course and for each meeting of the group you will need to bear the following things in mind:

I   Running the meeting

Aim

Each of the Growth courses has three, four or five sessions. At the beginning of the course, the aim is clearly stated. Before you do anything else, make sure that you are clear about the aim of the module and the aim of each session.

Content

Make sure you are familiar with the content of each session. Try to be reasonably familiar with all the material, especially the teaching input, so that you can lead the meeting without endlessly referring to the notes, and without your head being stuck in a book. But of course you will need these leaders' notes with you. That is what they are for!

Each group member also has a handout sheet for each session. This contains material that forms the basis of the group's work in this session. This book contains the leaders' notes plus photocopiable masters for a double-sided A4-handout for group members (these may also be downloaded from the CD-ROM). These usually need to be given out at the beginning of each meeting.

For some sessions, additional handouts are available, if you wish to use them. This is all clearly explained in the leaders' notes.

Method

We aim to use a variety of teaching methods. All the sessions in the Growth courses call for different ways of engaging with the material – teaching input from the leader, one-to-one discussion, splitting the group into the smaller units, presentations to one another and, in some courses, art and craft work. Do not shy away from using the more creative and experiential parts of the material. Despite initial embarrassment, many people will find these parts the most enjoyable and stimulating.

People learn in different ways. For some this will be through listening to the teaching input and reading what is on the handouts. For others it will be by appropriating the teaching input – reflecting it back in group discussions and making it their own. For others it will be by articulating their own insights, knowledge and experiences. For most of us it will be a combination of all these. Certainly, what people remember most from any group is what they say themselves. If for no other reason than this, we need to encourage discussion.

The courses aim at a creative dialogue between the tradition of the Church and our own experience of life. This is the way we will grow mature Christians who are able to live a Christian life in and for the world.

Leading the group

Two key words can help in effective leading of *Emmaus* groups, especially in this part of the course: conducting and empowering.

It is all too easy for the leader to feel too responsible and so end up doing everything. It is much better to see the leader's role as like that of the conductor of an orchestra. While working to a prepared script, members of a good orchestra put themselves, and thereby their own interpretation, into the music. For this to happen, individuals need to play to the best of their ability and to harmonize their contribution to the whole. Sometimes this is done by keeping silent. The task of the conductor is to draw out each contribution and to harmonize them, building something unique in the life of the group as a whole. This can be done by recognizing those who have gifts of hospitality, meditation, friendship, practical action, ability to create visual aids, teaching, etc. and allowing them to make their contribution. Equally, in discussion, different people will emerge with different contributions – some will see the connection with the Old Testament, others will only be interested in how it connects with life, someone else may have read widely and see connections in other ways. The good leader knows the instruments each person plays, and draws them out to enrich the whole. At any one session the good leader may not do any evident 'leading' – just as the conductor of an orchestra is the one person who does not play a musical instrument.

Empowering is the principle of helping people to believe in themselves, their value to God and to the group, and the worth of what they have to contribute. The task of the leader is not that of traditional teacher ('let me tell you the answer'), but that of helping others to make their own discoveries and to make the truth their own ('now I see', 'now I can . . .'). A good leader will help a group to break out of dependency into a creative group that takes responsibility and initiatives of its own – individually and together. It is important to watch for this, and to affirm all such steps whenever they emerge.

2   The people who make up the group

Any group consists of individuals, all with different needs and cares, all loved by God, and all at different points on the journey.

If your group is a new one and is coming together for the first time, you will need to take especial care over the first few meetings so that everyone gets to know everyone else and can share part of his or her own story. In the early meetings, building community is at least as important as covering the material. The introductory exercises in each of the sessions will be important here.

As the sessions go on and strangers begin to become friends, try to make sure everyone remains involved. This does not necessarily mean ensuring that everyone speaks, but it does mean that everyone is engaged. When planning the meetings ask yourself: Is there opportunity to speak, especially to ask a question? Is everyone able to make a contribution if they want to? You may need to try to contain people who are saying too much. Splitting the group up, or deliberately asking someone else's view, are two ways of handling this.

Difficult questions

One of the greatest fears for those leading a course like this is the fear of the difficult question. Some leaders deal with this by making it very hard for anyone to say anything. This is not the aim of *Emmaus*. The Growth courses are concerned to teach people the faith, but this is best done by encouraging questions and sharing experiences. If you do not know the answer to a question, say so. (However, you may also offer to come back with a response at the next session, which will allow you time to give the question some thought or ask the advice of others.)

Ask the rest of the group for suggestions. You are not expected to be the expert. You are expected to help others voice their questions and anxieties as they grow in faith.

For some questions, there may not be an answer. For many questions help can be available elsewhere in your church.

Care and support

Try to make sure people are cared for. Time spent at each meeting allowing people to unwind, get something off their chest or refer back to something that was discussed last week, is not time wasted. People need to feel they belong. Many people come to groups like this leaving behind them stressful situations at home or at work. Do not expect them to switch automatically on to our agenda. Allow people to bring their own agenda with them.

Remember that leaders are people too! If you are leading one of these Growth courses, whether you are ordained or lay, you will need some support, feedback and encouragement in that task. Having one or two people who will share in the leadership of the group and can encourage one another will help. So does being linked with and meeting regularly with the clergy and local church leaders. You do not need a lot of initial training to lead an *Emmaus* Growth course. But you do need a good level of ongoing support to be sustained in this ministry.

3 The practical maintenance of the group

Timing

Try to start and finish on time. The notes on timing in the tables assume a session of between one-and-a-half and one-and-three-quarter hours. With a cup of coffee, we are therefore talking about a two-hour meeting. Even if some people want to stay on longer than this, make sure it is OK to leave when the two hours are up. If people are experiencing stress at home about attending such a course, it is really important to keep to the deal about how long each session lasts.

You may well find, particularly with a relaxed and participative group, that there is more material than you have time to work through. On the one hand, it is important not to let the group ramble on, or for talkative people to talk too much. On the other hand, it is good to leave people feeling they could have gone on longer – and wanting more. Do not be afraid to adjust the amount of material you use to fit with your group – though make sure that the prayer/meditation time is not squeezed out.

Venue

Find the best venue for the meeting. For these courses this will probably be somebody's home. But it might not. Choose somewhere that is warm, comfortable and easy for everyone to get to.

Make sure there is enough seating and that the chairs are comfortable. Make sure that chairs are arranged in such a way that no one feels excluded.

The handouts

As well as the leaders' guide, this book contains photocopy masters for handouts for each Growth course. These are also available to download from the CD-ROM. You are entitled to make copies or download these pages for members of groups in your own church and the book is designed with this in mind. There is one main handout for every session of the course with some optional supplementary sheets.

Most groups will welcome the handouts and find them a valuable summary of each session. We suggest you provide everyone with a simple A4 ring binder to keep them in from week to week. It may help if the leader buys a hole-punch and supplies the sheets ready to slip into the file.

Some groups, however, will be 'paper-resistant' and may be thrown by having too many photocopied sheets to read and keep from week to week. Each course will work without handouts. You may need to provide scrap paper for some of the exercises and to reduce the teaching content in some of the sessions. Don't be afraid to go with the flow of the group and adapt the material to your own needs. That's what it's for.

If people need pencils, paper, Bibles, etc., make sure they know about this beforehand. Whenever possible, make sure you have spares with you for those who forget. Any other materials you need for a particular session are clearly marked in the leaders' notes.

Refreshments

Decide beforehand when you are going to have refreshments. Most groups have tea or coffee at the beginning or the end (or both!), but having refreshments at the beginning often means starting quite late and is therefore an invitation to arrive late! Having refreshments at the end can make the end of the meeting unclear and therefore make it hard for people to leave. You have to make your own decision on this, but how about refreshments in the middle? All the sessions call for some sort of group discussion. Why not set people to work on something, take orders for tea and coffee, and then give them their drinks in their groups. This does help time management.

Having a coffee break also offers the opportunity for the more relaxed, personal conversation that may prove vital in a person's faith journey.

These practical tasks of maintenance are very important. They can make or break a group. You may want to give responsibility for this to someone else. The group leader often has enough to worry about without also having to remember to buy the biscuits. You could ask someone to be the host for the group. This person could then be responsible for all these matters. Or have a co-leader who could learn about leading groups by working alongside the leader and taking charge of the practicalities.

4   Praying together

Prayer together is central to Christian maturity and central to these Growth courses. In these sessions, prayer is neither a perfunctory nod to God, nor merely a gathering together of what has been explored (though this is important), but it is an integral part of the learning process. If knowledge of God begins with reflection upon experience (ours and the Church's), and if it creates relationship with God that is nurtured by relationship with one another, then prayer must be at the very heart of all our seeking for God. Without prayer there can be no progress in our discipleship.

Give time for prayer in every session. This is clearly marked in the leaders' notes, but experience shows that sometimes it is the first thing to be squeezed out when time is short. Relegating prayer to the sidelines is the worst possible example of how to grow in discipleship.

Be bold in trying out the variety of methods of prayer that are suggested for these sessions. There is so much to be learned from the rich mosaic of Christian traditions. *Emmaus*, because it does not come from any one churchmanship tradition, aims to help people enter into a rich experience of Christian spirituality. More than anything else this will help people grow in their faith.

There are two great traditions of prayer in the Christian Church, liturgical and spontaneous. Both have proved of enduring value. It is good to build both into the prayer life of groups.

Liturgical prayer

As far as liturgical prayer is concerned, there are not only the services of Morning and Evening Prayer in *Common Worship* but there is also a growing number of versions of Compline (night prayer), and of various liturgical resources such as *Common Worship: Daily Prayer, New Patterns for Worship, Celebrating Common Prayer* and various Celtic resources. Most clergy will have a number of these. You do not have to use any form in its entirety, but from them you can draw appropriate patterns – and develop your own.

The important thing about liturgical prayer is to keep continuity so that people can rest back on the familiarity. Don't change it every week.

Spontaneous prayer

It often seems more difficult to help a group become comfortable with spontaneous prayer. Remember that no group, or person, is comfortable with anything until they are used to it; so determine to work through the awkward stage into enjoyment.

In helping people not used to praying out loud to begin to do so, it is important to remember that there are two hurdles most people find difficulty getting over. They are 'Will I get air time?' And 'Can I construct a prayer?'

There are ways we can give people 'air time' when they know they are the only ones allowed to pray at that time. Pass a book (Bible?) around a circle of people. Only the person holding the book can pray out loud. When you have prayed, pass the book on. If you do not want to pray aloud, simply pass the book on; but this is your chance.

There are ways of diminishing the sentence construction problem. Rather than saying, 'Let us thank God for his goodness to us by speaking out our praise,' simply say, 'We praise you for . . .' or 'We give thanks for . . .' and add the particular thing for which you want to praise/thank God. In intercession we can invite people to name people or a situation they want to pray for without having to construct a sentence. Because these prayers are single-word, or single-sentence prayers, they also greatly reduce concern about 'air time'.

5   **Goals**

In the task of leading a group, there are some greater goals that it is good to keep in mind, and some specific options which it is worth discussing with the leader of the local church. These additional goals are as follows.

Building community

We live in a world that is deeply fragmented, as much through social mobility as by the media, the telephone (and Internet) and the break-up of families. People are looking to belong, but are wary of commitment and of being organized or controlled. The Church has a great gift to give such a society. That gift is the Church itself, if it is living as God intends it to live, namely as an inclusive, empowering, faith community. A group doing the *Emmaus* course can become just that. It is important for the leader to look for ways of encouraging such an open and loving community to emerge through doing this course.

Building an engaging community

We follow Jesus Christ as Lord. He revealed himself as the incarnate one, the one who came into our world and lived his life among us, revealing God in the process. Any community that regards itself as Christian will, like Jesus Christ, also be engaged with the world around it. In all our sessions together, making connections with life must be an important goal of the leader. We must be alert to, and seeking to avoid, the danger Richard Foster highlights in his book, *Prayer,* when he says:

> Many of us today live in a kind of inner apartheid. We segregate out a small corner of pious activities and then can make no spiritual sense out of the rest of our lives.
>
> Richard Foster, *Prayer*

At every point we need to help the group to make the connection between faith and life. We can do this by:

■   *watching our language – checking each other whenever we use unnecessarily religious language ('how would you say that at school, in the supermarket, etc.?' is a good question to ask when we detect this going on);*

■   *considering the application ('how would this work out at home/work/in the pub?');*

■   *talking about the questions and objections others raise to our faith;*

■   *looking for ways of demonstrating our faith (offering to pray for those in need, holding a party or prayer vigil for someone or some need, doing a piece of service together).*

Building a worshipping community

One of the great forms of church life over the centuries has been the monastic movement. There are two things in its life of relevance to the building of the Church community today. One is worship, as T.S. Eliot put it:

> There is no life that is not in community,
> And no community not lived in praise of God.
>
> Choruses from 'The Rock'

which is why the prayer and worship elements of the group's life are so important. They build Christian community around the knowledge of God. It is important to keep our eye on that, and to look for ways to encourage that relaxed but real focus on God as the true centre of the group. The early chapters of Acts reveal an attractive church that had its life centred in the praise of God (2.11b, 46-47, 23-26; 10.44-46). It is also, of course, where the Emmaus story ends:

> And they worshipped him and returned to Jerusalem
> with great joy.
>
> Luke 24.52

To build community, it is vital to find ways of building the worship of God that are natural and appropriate to that group. It will repay careful and creative preparation.

In discovering appropriate patterns of prayer, symbols and musical contributions, it is good to look for patterns that can be repeated in the personal lives of group members. In this, group prayer and meditation should feed (and build upon) personal prayer.

Building a community lifestyle

The other thing that holds monastic orders together is their shared 'rule of life' – a commitment to practise certain things in a way which binds people together. The word 'rule' may not be a very helpful one today. A more helpful word, one that fits well with the whole concept of Emmaus, is 'way', as in the phrase 'a way of life' or 'lifestyle'. It can be a great help in building a faith community to develop together a specific way of life. Here is one such 'way of life' or 'shared lifestyle' that might emerge out of an Emmaus group:

We seek to follow Jesus Christ, by:

■   *making time to pray and meditate on God's word to us;*

■   *seeking to bless all whose lives we touch each day;*

■   *caring for each other in the group beyond our meeting times;*

■   *letting our faith affect the whole of our living.*

To sustain such a group lifestyle it would be important to meet regularly (once a month?), and honestly report successes, failures and next steps about our practice of this way of life.

It would be good to clarify with the church leader and with the group, whether – in the duration of this series of courses – there is a commitment to develop such a shared lifestyle. If you do, it will very likely grow out of the action sections at the end of each meeting, and will affect the way that you handle those parts of the programme.

In developing such a shared way of life it is good to remember the following points:

■   *Keep it to not more than half-a-dozen points (three to five is better).*

■   *Keep it as specific as possible.*

■   *Make it memorable (which will include making it as brief as possible).*

■   *Make the way you handle it a gift, not a drag or way of making people feel guilty.*

Leading a group of people who are seeking to grow in Christian faith can be in turns a daunting, stretching, frustrating, exciting, life-giving and joy-building experience. Each person who forms part of an *Emmaus* Growth group is infinitely precious to God. The task of guiding such a group is one of the great privileges of Christian life and ministry. It may sometimes seem an impossible thing for anyone to do well. But the God who calls us also equips us for the task, and to him be the glory.

What's new in the second edition?

We have taken the opportunity of this second edition to make the following changes:

- *Drawing on experience of the first edition, the text has been simplified in places.*

- *Some of the handouts have been reduced to two sheets of A4 for easier photocopying. They are also available to download from the CD-ROM.*

- *Page numbers have been removed from the members' handouts for churches that want to tackle the sessions in a different order.*

- *Extracts from the* Alternative Services Book *have been replaced with their equivalents from* Common Worship. *However, it remains very easy to adapt the handouts to the needs of different churches.*

- *All Bible quotations are now from the NRSV, the version which is now used across the Emmaus materials.*

Key to icons used in the leaders' notes and members' handouts

 Introduction to the session

 Suggestions for multi-media resources

 Action replay/reporting back

 Example timings for the session

 Buzz groups

 Suggestions for prayer

 Bible study

 Putting it into practice

 Input and discussion

part 01]

Living the gospel

Introduction

The aim of 'Living the gospel' is to make every small group in the church a dynamic and effective base for mission and every group member an effective witness for Christ. The course has been written for existing home groups; cells; for new groups being drawn together as a church engages with *Emmaus*; for those seeking to establish fresh expressions of church life; and for groups of new Christians who are beginning to grow.

You will need to be committed to the course over four meetings of your group and committed to the passages for study and the exercises in between.

Sharing the good news of Jesus Christ involves an investment of time as individuals and as a group. For this course to be worthwhile your group also needs to be prepared to invest fifteen to twenty minutes every two or three meetings, after the course finishes, in the whole business of witness and evangelism:

■ *reflecting on what has been happening;*

■ *holding one another to account;*

■ *praying together for those who do not know Christ;*

■ *planning and building stepping stones.*

Even though it may not be every week, this regular fifteen to twenty minute slot needs to become as much a part of your regular meeting as worship, Bible study and coffee time, if the principles contained here are to be worked out in practice and bear fruit for God's kingdom.

The principles contained in these notes are grounded in Scripture and the practice of the New Testament Church. They have been put into practice in different parts of the world and are proving effective in evangelism in many different places.

Outline of sessions

The four sessions of the course will help you to look at:

■ *Understanding: Understanding your* oikos

■ *Prayer: Praying for your* oikos

■ *Service: Serving your* oikos

■ *Building stepping stones to faith*

Oikos is a Greek word and means 'extended household' or 'network of relationships'. 'Living the gospel' is about helping each other to communicate Christian faith in our own *oikos* or relationship network.

Preparing the group

The course is designed for groups meeting weekly or fortnightly and assumes that the group members already know each other well. If they don't, then take time for introductions in the first meeting. We've also assumed that the group wants to become more effective in sharing its faith as individuals and as a group. There is no teaching here on why we should be involved in sharing our faith or on the content of the Christian gospel. Depending on the group, you may need to build in sessions on the 'Why' and 'What' of evangelism before coming on to the 'How'.

You will also need the agreement of the group members to take them down this road, and of the leadership of your church. If 'Living the gospel' is to be effective, it will probably mean change in individual lives and the life of the group.

Relating to the wider Church

'Living the gospel' assumes that your church has a structure in place for evangelism and nurture through groups or one-to-one visiting. In other words, you are committed to *Emmaus* or to some similar way of engaging with evangelism. The course aims to equip members of your group to pray for, serve and witness to their network of family and friends and to seek to draw some of them to the point where they want to learn more about the Christian faith. That 'learning more' can then take place within the context of nurture groups.

If the whole church is developing 'stepping stones' for evangelism, alongside the work being done by the small groups, then this will obviously help.

What is envisaged here is not that the business of sharing the faith with enquirers should happen in the 'normal' group meetings, (which continue to be for building up and supporting committed Christians in their own discipleship). The vision is that evangelism and outreach become a natural part of the life of your group and of every group member.

Leading the meetings

Each session is designed to last 90 minutes and fit within a 'normal' group session. No suggestions have been made in this module for worship, coffee or a wider prayer time – those can just happen as normal and in the pattern you have evolved. The sessions are timed to 75 minutes, to give space for worship and prayer, but be flexible to the needs of the group and to what is going well.

Some preparation of leading the Bible study is needed by the leader, but not a great deal of skill or head knowledge. The most important thing is that the leaders of the group are willing to set an example in praying for, serving and witnessing to your network of relationships and to encourage others to do the same.

Support for the leader

In seeking to equip others for faith sharing and seeking to transform your group into a base for this, you are placing yourself on the front line of Christian ministry. Make sure there are two or three committed people praying for you and your family during the period of the course. Pray yourself for the members of your group and ask other groups in the church to support your own group in prayer. You may be helped in your own preparation by reading *Contact* and having this available for the rest of the group.

To be able to equip members of your group to share their faith effectively and fruitfully and to see people regularly coming to faith through the witness of your group is a bold, worthwhile and significant vision in itself. If small groups all over your church and all over the country can also become bases for effective evangelism and faith sharing, then we will see not only groups and individual lives changed but also whole churches, communities and cities.

Acknowledgements

The material used here as part of *Emmaus* is mainly adapted from material developed in different places around the world in Korea, North America and Italy – particularly by Paul Yong y Cho, Carl George, Ralph Neighbour and Mgr Perini.

Additional resources

For more information on the way in which evangelism is developing across the Churches, see *Evangelism in a Spiritual Age* (Yvonne Richmond, Nick Spencer, Rob Frost, Anne Richards, Mark Ireland, Steven Croft, Church House Publishing, 2004) and John Finney, *Emerging Evangelism* (Darton, Longman & Todd, 2004).

For more help and information on building mission-centred small groups in your church, see Steven Croft, *Transforming Communities*, (Darton, Longman & Todd, 2002).

For more information and practical help on developing fresh expressions of church life see the Fresh Expressions web site: www.freshexpressions.org.uk.

Session One: Understanding your *oikos*

	mins
Buzz groups: Pictures of evangelism	15
Bible study: *Oikos* in the New Testament	30
Buzz groups: Discover your *oikos*	25
Putting it into practice	5

Session Two: Praying for your *oikos*

	mins
Buzz groups: Your journey to faith	20
Bible study: The journey	15
Bible study: Prayer and the journey	15
Group activity: Beginning to pray	15
Prayer together	10
Putting it into practice	5

Session Three: Serving your *oikos*

	mins
Buzz groups: Experiences of prayer	20
Bible study: Serving others	30
Buzz groups: Serving your *oikos*	30
Putting it into practice	5

Session Four: Building stepping stones to faith

	mins
Buzz groups: How did it go?	20
Bible study: Witnesses and stepping stones	30
Buzz groups: Building stepping stones to faith	30
Putting it into practice	5

Understanding your *oikos*

Buzz groups: Pictures of evangelism

Take a few moments to welcome people and give an overview of the aim of the course. Explain why you are taking part in *Emmaus* as a group and what you hope and pray the results will be.

Allow about 20 minutes for the sharing time under the headings given on the members' handout. Be aware that for many Christians 'evangelism' is something that makes them feel guilty and inadequate. Give people permission to share that. You may like to draw the sharing together with an all-together time in which you briefly remind people of why we are called to share our faith.

Bible study: *Oikos* in the New Testament

This is the time to explain the word *oikos* – the Greek word meaning 'extended household' or network of relationships. In describing how the gospel spreads along these networks, try to give some personal illustrations from the life of the group.

If your group is not used to reading aloud then ask people to prepare the passages in advance.

- *Mark 1.14-18*   *A network of brothers and cousins*

- *Mark 1.29-30*   *From there to the mother-in-law and extended community*

- *Mark 2.13-17*   *Levi is converted and asks his* oikos *to dinner with Jesus*

- *Mark 5.19-20*   *The former demoniac is commanded to go and tell his* oikos

- *Mark 6.8-10*   *The disciples are commanded to be* oikos-*based in their outreach*

Draw things together with two final questions:

- *Can you begin to see the principle of* oikos *evangelism?*

- *Can you think of any other New Testament passages where the principle applies?*

If you have time, look briefly at Paul in Philippi – at the conversion of Lydia and the jailer (Acts 16).

Buzz groups: Discover your *oikos*

You will need to prepare scrap paper and pens.

Take time to introduce the exercise – stressing its purpose and relevance. (Before we can witness to our *oikos*, we have to find out who the people are in our own network.) Then take the group step by step through building a picture (see members' handout). Try to be as light-hearted as you can and emphasize that it doesn't have to be complete at this stage. There will be a chance in the week to go back over things and make a 'fair copy'.

Some people may be embarrassed at not knowing many people at all. Be sensitive and affirming here. Some may feel guilty at not knowing many non-Christians. Allow folk to draw their own conclusions about this. Everyone, Christians and non-Christians, should be noted down at this stage.

Take about ten minutes to build the basic *oikos* picture, then allow five minutes for sharing in pairs and a further ten minutes for questions and discussion. The final three questions can be answered in pairs and then discussed as a whole group. As you draw to a close, look forward over the next few weeks and give an overview of the next three sessions (prayer; service; witness). Also, if you can, ask one member of the group to share the story of how he or she came to the Christian faith and note as a group what part *oikos* members played in this.

Putting it into practice

End the session by looking forward to the Putting it into practice section on the handout and the Bible readings. Lead into a time of open prayer and commitment to mission. The assignments in between group meetings are a very important part of the course. Encourage people to take them seriously. This one will need about an hour to complete prayerfully and carefully. You will need to give out the handouts and encourage people to bring them back completed for next time.

Bible reading

There are seven passages between meetings. That doesn't mean you can't meet fortnightly!

The Bible study is less important than the assignment, but it is still helpful if people can make time.

Summary and example timings

	mins
Buzz groups: Pictures of evangelism	15
Bible study: *Oikos* in the New Testament	30
Buzz groups: Discover your *oikos*	25
Putting it into practice	5

Understanding your *oikos*

Pictures of evangelism

Talk together in small groups about your experience of sharing the Christian faith:

- ■ *In organized 'missions' and events.*

- ■ *In informal friendships and contacts.*

- ■ *Has this faith sharing been a positive or negative experience for you and those you have talked with?*

- ■ *Has it been effective in terms of seeing people come to faith?*

- ■ *If so – why? If not – why not?*

Oikos in the New Testament

In the New Testament, much of the evangelism is based on the *oikos* – a network of existing relationships.

Mark 1.14-18

> Now after John was arrested, Jesus came to Galilee, proclaiming the good news of God, and saying, 'The time is fulfilled, and the kingdom of God has come near; repent, and believe in the good news.' As Jesus passed along the Sea of Galilee, he saw Simon and his brother Andrew casting a net into the sea – for they were fishermen. And Jesus said to them, 'Follow me and I will make you fish for people.' And immediately they left their nets and followed him.

Mark 1.29-30

> As soon as they left the synagogue, they entered the house of Simon and Andrew, with James and John. Now Simon's mother-in-law was in bed with a fever, and they told him about her at once.

Mark 2.13-17

> Jesus went out again beside the sea; the whole crowd gathered around him, and he taught them. As he was walking along, he saw Levi son of Alphaeus sitting at the tax booth, and he said to him, 'Follow me.' And he got up and followed him. And as he sat at dinner in Levi's house, many tax collectors and sinners were also sitting with Jesus and his disciples – for there were many who followed him. When the scribes of the Pharisees saw that he was eating with sinners and tax collectors, they said to his disciples, 'Why does he eat with tax collectors and sinners?' When Jesus heard this, he said to them, 'Those who are well have no need of a physician, but those who are sick; I have come to call not the righteous but sinners.'

Mark 5.19-20

> But Jesus refused and said to him, 'Go home to your friends, and tell them how much the Lord has done for you, and what mercy he has shown you.' And he went away and began to proclaim in the Decapolis how much Jesus had done for him; and everyone was amazed.

Mark 6.8-10

> He ordered them to take nothing for their journey except a staff; no bread, no bag, no money in their belts; but to wear sandals and not to put on two tunics. He said to them, 'Wherever you enter a house, stay there until you leave the place.'

Discover your *oikos*

Find a pen and paper.

- *Write your name in the centre.*

- *Above your name write the names of your extended family with whom you are in meaningful contact: spouse; children; parents; uncles; cousins; grandchildren, etc.*

- *Below your name write the names of your neighbours and people in your community you know well.*

- *To the right of your name write the names of your work colleagues or people you know through work.*

- *To the left of your name write the names of your friends and people you know through hobbies, sports, etc.*

Do two more things:

- *Put a * by everyone who is already a Christian.*

- *Underline the people with whom you spend at least 30 minutes a week in face-to-face contact or conversation (the 30 minutes doesn't have to be all at the same time).*

For the purpose of this course, the people whose names you have underlined are your *oikos*.

Now compare notes with the people sitting either side of you.

As a whole group answer three further questions:

- *As a group we have an oikos of ___ people.*

- *As a church we have an oikos of ___ people.*

- *To draw these people to Christ we need to _____.*

Putting it into practice

Before the next group meeting write out a neater copy of your *oikos* on the supplementary handout provided.

Pray once for every member of your *oikos*. Listen to anything God says to you about them.

Bible reading

Spot the *oikos* principle at work.

Acts 10.1-48   Acts 16.11-15   Acts 16.22-34   Acts 17.1-9

Acts 18.1-11   Acts 28.1-11   Acts 28.30-31

Emmaus Growth course handout: Understanding your oikos

Understanding your *oikos*

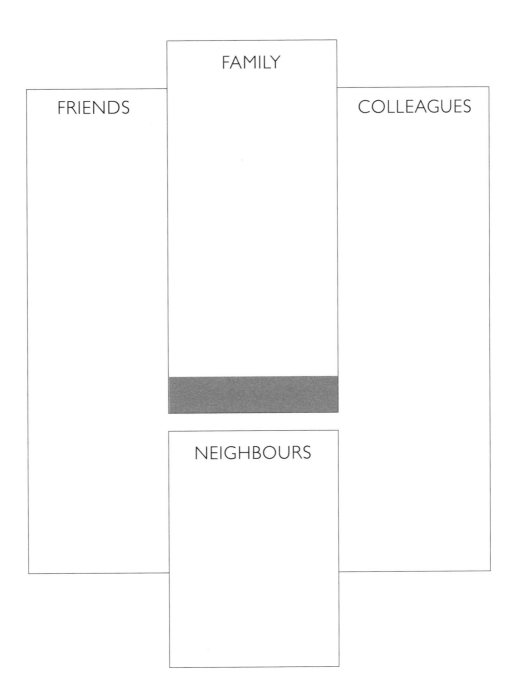

FAMILY

FRIENDS

COLLEAGUES

NEIGHBOURS

Praying for your *oikos*

Buzz groups: Your journey to faith

A testimony would be a good way to introduce the meeting and the time of sharing. The first part of the sharing exercise is best done as a whole group to check that people are OK so far. Invite the group to review their thinking since you last met:

How did you get on with the passages?

Did you change your *oikos* in revising it?

Then divide into smaller groups of three or four to talk together about how people became Christians:

■   *What were the main stages on your journey to faith?*

■   *Who helped you and prayed for you?*

■   *Were any books or speakers helpful and significant?*

Encourage the group to be careful in listening to each other and encouraging and affirming one another's stories.

Even if the group has been together through the *Emmaus* Nurture course, it is still worth engaging with this sharing exercise.

Bible study: The journey

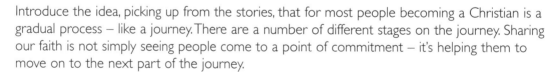

The length of time you take for this section will depend on how familiar people are with the idea of coming to faith as a journey and their part in the journey. It does need to be grasped by the group as a whole before you can move on. If your group has already taken part in different sections of *Emmaus* then the journey picture will not be new. However, if you are an established house group in a church that is just beginning to use *Emmaus*, then this is a very important idea to get across.

Introduce the idea, picking up from the stories, that for most people becoming a Christian is a gradual process – like a journey. There are a number of different stages on the journey. Sharing our faith is not simply seeing people come to a point of commitment – it's helping them to move on to the next part of the journey.

Look together at the story of the two sons in Luke 15.11-32. It is possible to find seven 'stages' on the journey of the younger brother and one stage for the elder. Ask the group to see how many it can find and write them down on the members' handout with a parallel situation in people's lives today. Rembrandt's painting of the return of the prodigal son has become very popular in recent years as a tool for reflection on the story, largely because of Henri Nouwen's meditation *The Return of the Prodigal Son*. It may be helpful to have a copy of the picture for the session.

Give some time for people to engage with the study in small groups, then go through your answers together. The supplementary handout, which is an extract from Steven Croft's book,

Growing New Christians, may be help you in your own preparation, or it may be useful to give out to the group. In leading this part of the session, it may be helpful for the women in the group to acknowledge that this is a story about three men and to give the opportunity to ask what difference it makes to read this story as a woman.

Bible study: Prayer and the journey

Before thinking about prayer you may like to ask people whether they pray regularly for those who are not Christians at the present time. If so, how do they pray?

You'll need to study the passages on prayer fairly carefully before the meeting. There may be other texts you want to introduce here – or insights from your personal experience of seeing others come to faith.

Luke 6.12-16 – The choosing of the twelve

Jesus is engaged in the same activity we are concerned with: calling and making disciples. Before he calls the twelve to him he spends the night in prayer. We can have no doubt that he would have spent an extensive time praying for them before he even invited them to follow. Praying for others is following Jesus' example.

Colossians 4.12-14 – Epaphras

Epaphras' concern is for his Christian friends left behind in Colossae. Paul describes his prayer for the people there as like wrestling: the Greek word is *agonizai* – from which we take our word 'agonize'. Praying for others is hard work.

Galatians 4.17-20 – Paul and the Galatians

Paul uses the image of a mother giving birth to describe the pain and the hard labour he is passing through in prayer on behalf of the converts in Galatia who are slipping away from faith. But note that he writes that 'I am again in the pain of childbirth'. By inference he has been through this kind of prayer once already, around the time at which the Galatians came to faith.

Group activity: Beginning to pray

Work through the exercise on the handout. Give people plenty of time in the meeting to think about who to pray for – it's the kind of thing that we all tend to put off if it's left to 'homework'. After they have made an initial selection, suggest . they share their list in triplets and say a little about it (and the process of choosing the names). There's no objection to anyone having more than six names or bucking the system!

Then invite people to get together with two others in the group and exchange one or two names each (each person chooses which).

You should give some thought before the meeting to the prayer triplets. People are going to be meeting within the group in these triplets on a regular basis. They may be better as planned groups rather than randomly selected.

If the triplets want to meet outside the main group time, that's fine – but there is no expectation of that in the course.

Prayer together

After people have talked about the names on their lists in triplets, it may be appropriate to have a brief time of silent or spoken prayer in these groups of three as each person is named before God and everyone prays for them.

Putting it into practice

The action and Bible reading will need some introduction and explanation. Look forward briefly to the next session and then end with your normal time of prayer.

Summary and example timings

	mins
Buzz groups: Your journey to faith	20
Bible study: The journey	15
Bible study: Prayer and the journey	15
Group activity: Beginning to pray	15
Prayer together	10
Putting it into practice	5

Your journey to faith

- *How did you get on with the passages?*

- *Did you change your oikos in revising it?*

Think about how you became a Christian:

- *What were the main stages on your journey to faith?*

- *Who helped you and prayed for you?*

- *Were any books or speakers helpful and significant?*

The journey

For most people, becoming a Christian is a gradual process – like a journey. There are a number of different stages on the journey. Sharing our faith is not simply a matter of seeing people come to a point of commitment – it's helping them to move on to the next stage.

Look at the story of the two sons in Luke 15.11-32.

It is possible to find seven 'stages' on the journey of the younger brother and one stage for the elder. See how many you can find. Write them down on the table overleaf and write a parallel situation in people's lives today.

Prayer and the journey

The main way we can help others move forward in their journey is to pray for them. Read aloud these passages about prayer and 'moving on'. For each one, see what you can learn about prayer for the people you know:

Luke 6.12-16 – The choosing of the twelve

> Now during those days he went out to the mountain to pray; and he spent the night in prayer to God. And when day came, he called his disciples and chose twelve of them, whom he also named apostles: Simon, whom he named Peter, and his brother Andrew, and James, and John, and Philip, and Bartholomew, and Matthew, and Thomas, and James son of Alphaeus, and Simon, who was called the Zealot, and Judas son of James, and Judas Iscariot, who became a traitor.

Colossians 4.12-14 – Epaphras – 'who is one of you'

> Epaphras, who is one of you, a servant of Christ Jesus, greets you. He is always wrestling in his prayers on your behalf, so that you may stand mature and fully assured in everything that God wills. For I testify for him that he has worked hard for you and for those in Laodicea and in Hierapolis. Luke, the beloved physician, and Demas greet you.

1	
2	
3	
4	
5	
6	
7	
8	

Galatians 4.17-20 – Paul and the Galatians

> They make much of you, but for no good purpose; they want to exclude you, so that you may make much of them. It is good to be made much of for a good purpose at all times, and not only when I am present with you. My little children, for whom I am again in the pain of childbirth until Christ is formed in you, I wish I were present with you now and could change my tone, for I am perplexed about you.

Beginning to pray

Most of us find it hard to pray regularly for a great number of people. This exercise helps you discern who to pray for in your *oikos*:

- *In a time of quiet, look prayerfully through the names in your oikos.*

- *Prayerfully select three to six people from that list to be the focus of regular prayer, service and witness.*

- *Write their names on a simple card and keep it in your Bible or diary.*

Choosing the names

Deciding who to pray for regularly is between you and God. The following suggestions may be helpful.

- *All should be people with whom you spend a reasonable time in face-to-face contact each week.*

- *Try to include at least one person you do not like or get on with (Jesus tells us to love our enemies and pray for our persecutors).*

- *Try to include at least one person who is a long way from the kingdom (Jesus focused his time and attention on those who were 'sinners', those whom religious people had given up on).*

- *Try to include at least one person in whom you can see God working at the present time.*

All these categories may overlap.

Get together with two others in your group and exchange one or two names each (you choose which). Write these names down on the prayer list.

Putting it into practice

There should be up to ten names on your prayer list: six from your *oikos* and four from your prayer partners.

Try to pray each day for the ten names on your own prayer list.

Ask God to show you how to pray for each one. Remember that prayer is always about listening as well as speaking to God.

Bible reading

Some principles of prayer:

Matthew 5.43-48	Matthew 21.18-22
Matthew 6.1-15	John 16.19-24
Matthew 7.7-12	Acts 4.23-31
Matthew 18.19-20	

Praying for your *oikos*

The story of the two sons

1   Running away

'A few days later the younger son gathered all he had and travelled to a distant country . . .'

Many people begin their story by running away from the love of their heavenly Father. Perhaps in the teenage years, perhaps later, there is a flight from God; a rebellion against him. For some the rebellion is active. My wife was brought up a Roman Catholic and actively rebelled against the things her school and parents and friends had taught her in her early teens. It was six or seven years before she began her journey back to God again. For others the rebellion is passive. We just slip away. We can't be bothered to find out more. In all those years of rebellion we know, deep down inside, that God is there; we know the way we should go; we know what he expects. We think we can do better on our own. So, whether actively or by default, we set off or drift off in the opposite direction. We travel to a far country and there we stay, without so much as a phone call or a postcard home.

2   Living far away, having a good time

'There he squandered his property in dissolute living.'

This is the point in the journey which many, many people in our society and culture have reached, and there they remain for many years. As surely as the younger son knew his father was there but made no attempt to contact him, so the vast majority of people in our society believe in God but want nothing to do with him other than at their convenience. All the wealth which people have been given: all of their love, their talents, the resources of their lives, the years which will never return, is squandered on pleasures which are short-lived. There people settle and there they often remain until they begin to be in need.

3   Sensing your need of your heavenly Father

'When he had spent everything, a severe famine took place throughout that country, and he began to be in need . . . But when he came to himself he said . . .'

Time after time, what prompts people to move on in a spiritual journey is an awareness of need in some form or another. It was not until the younger son's natural resources ran out that he began to think about his father. Even then, because of his pride, he attempted to meet his own need by every means possible, even lowering himself to feed the pigs, before need drove him, in the end to turn for home.

So often similar factors are operating today. People are shaken out of their self-sufficiency by some spiritual or emotional need and at those times begin to seek God. It may be a bereavement; a problem in a relationship; a mid-life crisis; weakened health and the sure knowledge that death is approaching; achieving life's goals and realizing there must be something more; depression of some kind; an awareness that you cannot bring up children by human standards. From time to time in all our lives we are brought face to face with our own frailty, our humanity and our need for God. It is at those times that we reach out and look for him and at those times especially that he is searching for us.

4 Turning round to come back

> 'I will get up and go to my father, and I will say to him, "Father, I have sinned against heaven and before you; I am no longer worthy to be called your son; treat me like one of your hired hands."'

A common point on the journey, after a person has realised their need for God, is the turning round to come back to him. Conversion means, literally, turning round, a change of direction. Conversion in this sense means the point at which you stop travelling away from God and begin the journey home. In a person's life it may be marked by very simple things: a desire to have a child baptised; or to begin attending church; a willingness to talk to Christians (if they know any) and to ask questions. The first steps are often very tentative. There is still some way to go before a point of commitment is reached, but the change of direction has already happened. It is at this point, very often, that a person will be ready to take part in an enquirers' or nurture group.

5 On your way home.

> 'So he set off and went to his father.'

Those words contain a whole story in themselves. The son was in a distant country. The journey home would be neither short nor easy. Perhaps there were many distractions and stumbling blocks along the way; many times when the son's fear and shame at meeting his father outweighed his desire to be at home and he thought of turning back. In John Bunyan's story of the journey, The Pilgrim's Progress, Christian has a whole series of encounters between his meeting with Evangelist and laying down his burden at the foot of the cross. For most people today, after the initial desire to turn round and seek God will come a looking and a learning and a discovering of the faith. The journey back is not, generally, the work of a moment. Help and guidance is needed each step of the way.

6 In the arms of your father

> 'But while he was still far off, his father saw him and was filled with compassion; he ran and put his arms around him and kissed him. Then the son said to him, "Father . . ."'

The best part of the story is the picture of the gracious father still looking down the road after all of these years of his younger son being away. After the journey home, after the looking and the learning, comes the time for commitment and reconciliation of the person seeking God with the God who has been seeking him or her. It is one of the richest privileges of ministry to share in the joy of those times of reconciliation and commitment as person after person comes home to God. It is also very important, to change the metaphor to another Jesus uses, that people come to this new birth in a right and helpful way and that we are effective spiritual midwives. There is more joy in heaven over one sinner who repents . . .

7   Taking your place in the family

The son comes home and there is reconciliation, feasting and a great celebration. If we take Jesus' story into the future, what would happen after the party is over? Things would not be as they were before when the son was at home. The younger son now needs to take his place again as a member of the family. He and his father will have much to talk about. He needs to work out his relationships to other members of the family. No doubt also, he needs to find his own place again in the work of the family on the farm. All of this will take time.

The parallels with our inner journey back to God are obvious. After a person has come home to the Father, there is and should be a period of rejoicing, not only for them but for the Church or the small group. But then comes the period of taking his or her place as a member of the family once again; of deepening his or her relationship with God; of growing in relationship with older brothers and sisters; of beginning to find a place within the work of the family. As much help and care is needed at this stage of the journey as at any other.

8   Playing the part of the elder brother

There is one other place in the story we may find ourselves again and again in our Christian lives, and that is in the place of the elder brother. He has lived at home so long that he now takes everything for granted. Everything that the father has is his. Yet his relationship with his father has declined and degenerated to one of work and service rather than love.

As Jesus tells the story, we are not told what happens to the elder brother. We leave him sulking outside the banquet, too proud to come in. Jesus means us to ask ourselves the question, will we enter into a fresh experience of the Father's love; or will we stay outside, sullen, jealous and angry; living among such riches but in reality so poor?

There are so many Christians, among them many who have worked hard in ministry, who find themselves in the elder brother's place in the story. Like the Ephesian Church we have laboured long and hard for the kingdom but we have lost our first love (Revelation 2.4). Part of the journey for those involved with nurturing new Christians will be discovering yourself in the elder brother's shoes and choosing once again to join the party. Part of caring for new Christians will be discovering that, surprisingly quickly, people can 'graduate' to being elder brothers, unable to recognise that other people are now the focus of the attention, joy and celebration which they so recently enjoyed.

Part of the challenge for any church which is experiencing significant growth and numbers of adults coming to faith is enabling the elder brothers and younger brothers to understand each other and to work together.

From Steven Croft, *Growing New Christians*, CPAS/Marshall Pickering, 1993 pp.19–24.

–

Serving your *oikos*

Buzz groups: Experiences of prayer

Reflect together on your experiences of prayer following the questions on the handout.

It will probably be best to reflect together as one group rather than in huddles or pairs. Adapt the questions as best you can to the needs of your particular group. Be aware that the exercise will raise some fairly deep questions about people's own prayer life (or lack of). If this is a significant problem for the whole group, then perhaps you need a couple of sessions after this course on building a discipline of prayer. The *Emmaus* course 'Growing in prayer' in *Growing as a Christian* may be a good one to tackle next.

The final question of the sharing time is meant to provide a lead into the discussion that follows.

Bible study: Serving others

If your group has done any thinking or courses before on personal evangelism, what has happened so far will be fairly familiar – and may even result in some yawns.

This third session, however, is very different and very radical to most small groups and Christians. There are two central ideas in the Bible study and the exercise that follows:

1   To serve others is an essential part of evangelism. We cannot simply make the leap from praying to talking.

2   We need as much help (if not more) in serving and loving others as we need in praying for them and talking to them.

The principal help provided here is accountability: giving account to one another of the ways we have tried to be a servant in the past week.

Once this principle of service as an essential part of witness is accepted, several things follow:

■   *This aspect of faith sharing is something everyone can do.*

■   *Witness is about the whole way we live our lives (not just the things we say in 'church mode').*

■   *We are all at the same level, however much we know about Christianity.*

Growing in our service of others is far more about character and gradual growth in becoming like Christ than a special burst of activity. We need to be very sure what motivates us. However, particular exercises can help to build habits and character.

You should plan a short input at the beginning of the Bible study to communicate the point of being a servant to members of our *oikos* and then go into the study as outlined.

Jesus came not to be served but to serve. He calls and challenges us to be servants of others.

Read John 13.1-17 together and follow through the exercise on the handout.

The best way to understand the passage is to act it out. Appoint a man and a woman from the group to wash feet (they should be volunteers). The man should wash the feet of the other men in the group and the woman should wash the feet of the women. Alternatively, the group could agree to wash one another's hands.

You will need to prepare towels, bowls of water and soap in advance. Those wearing tights – or those who are very embarrassed – should be excused. Allow a few moments of quiet after the foot washing, then talk together, following the questions on the handout.

A great deal could come out of the passage for the ongoing life of the group. Service needs to be modelled within the body of Christ as well as Christians serving those outside.

Then talk together:

- *What were the feelings of the foot washers?*

- *What were the feelings of those whose feet were washed?*

- *Which verses from the passage speak most to you?*

- *How do members of this group serve one another?*

- *Make a list on a large sheet of paper.*

- *How could members of this group serve one another?*

- *Make another list. Jot down the ideas from both lists.*

Buzz groups: Serving your *oikos*

You may need a short break between the Bible study and the exercise. Why not have coffee in the middle of the meeting instead of at the beginning or end tonight? After the break take a few minutes to go through the exercise with the whole group before beginning the first stage, which is individual reflection. You'll need some pens and scrap paper.

As part of your preparation for leading the meeting, it may help you to go through the exercise (see members' handout) with just one other person a week in advance, so that you can share with the rest of the group how you found things.

The second part of the exercise is meant to be very specific. There may be some resistance here either to the idea of accountability or the idea of serving others (or the latter may be disguised as the former). Avoid giving the impression that anyone has to do anything. All you can do is encourage each other – but this kind of accountability is meant to be part of Christian discipleship.

Putting it into practice

This should be a time for encouragement! Be sure to place the emphasis on doing as well as praying.

Bible reading

The readings this week will be particularly helpful as people seek to put into practice what they have been learning.

Summary and example timings

	mins
Buzz groups: Experiences of prayer	20
Bible study: Serving others	30
Buzz groups: Serving your *oikos*	30
Putting it into practice	5

Experiences of prayer

Reflect together on your experiences of prayer:

- *Was it easy to pray in a disciplined way each day?*

- *Did you see any answers to prayer in the first week?*

- *Did you find the Bible passages helpful in showing you how to pray?*

- *Were you inspired to do anything as a result of the prayer?*

Serving others

The first step in 'Living the gospel' is to pray for members of your *oikos* regularly.

The second step is not to talk to them about your faith!

The second step is to love them and to serve them.

Jesus came not to be served but to serve. He calls and challenges us to be servants of others.

Read John 13.1-17

Now before the festival of the Passover, Jesus knew that his hour had come to depart from this world and go to the Father. Having loved his own who were in the world, he loved them to the end. The devil had already put it into the heart of Judas son of Simon Iscariot to betray him. And during supper Jesus, knowing that the Father had given all things into his hands, and that he had come from God and was going to God, got up from the table, took off his outer robe, and tied a towel around himself. Then he poured water into a basin and began to wash the disciples' feet and to wipe them with the towel that was tied around him. He came to Simon Peter, who said to him, 'Lord, are you going to wash my feet?' Jesus answered, 'You do not know now what I am doing, but later you will understand.' Peter said to him, 'You will never wash my feet.' Jesus answered, 'Unless I wash you, you have no share with me.' Simon Peter said to him, 'Lord, not my feet only but also my hands and my head!' Jesus said to him, 'One who has bathed does not need to wash, except for the feet, but is entirely clean. And you are clean, though not all of you.' For he knew who was to betray him; for this reason he said, 'Not all of you are clean.' After he had washed their feet, had put on his robe, and had returned to the table, he said to them, 'Do you know what I have done to you? You call me Teacher and Lord – and you are right, for that is what I am. So if I, your Lord and Teacher, have washed your feet, you also ought to wash one another's feet. For I have set you an example, that you also should do as I have done to you. Very truly, I tell you, servants are not greater than their master, nor are messengers greater than the one who sent them. If you know these things, you are blessed if you do them.'

Serving your *oikos*

The aim of this exercise is to help you begin to see how to serve your *oikos*.

- *Take some time in the quietness to look through each name on your list. Jot down on a piece of scrap paper their different needs and how you could serve them in practical ways.*

- *Get together in the same triplet as last week. Share your ideas about serving different members of your oikos. Help each other as much as you can.*

After you have talked in general about your list, then be specific.

- *Take the names you have asked others to pray for.*

- *In discussion in the triplet, identify one definite practical way you can serve each person in the coming week, e.g. wash their car; give them a lift; fetch the sandwiches; babysit.*

- *Write down that suggestion and commitment for your own names and for the other four.*

- *Pray together for each person and your commitment to serve them.*

Discuss any questions, problems or challenges in the whole group.

Putting it into practice

Continue to pray for the people on your prayer list each day. Pray that God will draw them to himself.

Pray also for your two prayer partners as they begin to serve their *oikos*.

Begin to serve your own *oikos*!

Bible reading

About being a servant:

Isaiah 42.1-4

Matthew 20.20-28

Luke 16.10-15

Romans 1.1-6

Romans 12.1-21

1 Corinthians 13

Philippians 2.1-13

Building stepping stones to faith

Buzz groups: How did it go?

Pray hard for the group this week in between meetings and pray that everyone comes back for week four!

It may help to begin with the whole group together and to share some of your own experiences (including the failures). Emphasize again that these first steps are part of continuing to build habits and character. Then ask people to divide into triplets and look together at the questions on the handout.

■ *Have there been any significant answers to prayer?*

■ *Have you been able to keep to the discipline of praying regularly?*

■ *Describe your experiences of serving in the way you planned last time.*

■ *Has anything happened in you or in others as a result of the serving?*

Suggest that the triplets spend most of their time talking about acts of service and sharing what happened rather than the prayer. After the discussion has run its course for a while, invite each triplet to sum up for the whole group.

Bible study: Witnesses and stepping stones

There are two parts to the Bible study. Introduce the first passage by summing up what has happened so far and describe these three steps to being a witness:

■ *Step 1 in 'Living the gospel' is to pray for your oikos.*

■ *Step 2 is to love and serve your oikos.*

■ *Step 3 is to be a witness as best you can.*

Responding to questions

Not all of us have the gift of evangelism – but we are all called to be witnesses. As we pray for people and serve people, they may begin to ask us questions.

Read 1 Peter 3.15-16 together. Spend a few minutes thinking about what it means. Then role play the verses in pairs in a work situation. One person should be the Christian. The other should be the *oikos* member for whom you are praying, and should ask interested questions about the hope in the Christian.

As a whole group, think of some principles for helpful things to say in that kind of situation. Write them down together.

It's worth spending a little bit of time making the distinction between being an evangelist and being a witness. The New Testament makes it clear that only some people have the spiritual gift of evangelism. They will be the ones who are frequently used by God to communicate the Christian faith – even to people they don't know very well. It may be worth asking the group if they can spot anyone with this gift in your group or in your church. However, all of us are called to be witnesses – to bear witness to what God has done in our lives at appropriate times.

I Peter 3.15-16 are verses for witnesses to study, learn and act out. Emphasize that, as we pray and serve our *oikos*, then God will give us opportunities to speak for him and give a positive witness to faith.

The role play may be difficult for some people. Depending on your group, give people permission to 'pass' and just talk about the passage as it applies to their 'real' situation.

Building stepping stones

Read I Corinthians 9.19-23. The study of the passage should be fairly brief. It should aim to give a biblical foundation for the principle of reaching out to people where they are and building stepping stones to faith. The more this can be earthed in your experience and in the experience of others in the group, the better.

Buzz groups: Building stepping stones to faith

If you are running short of time in this session, don't try to do the whole exercise. Focus on the stepping stones for individuals this time (see members' handout) and then devote the whole of the next meeting to reflecting on what people have learned from the course; deciding on where you go from here as a group and thinking about the stepping stones you can build together.

The first part of the exercise should be done in triplets. The ideas of service are important – the vision now is to build this dimension of caring for others into our whole lives.

The second and third parts of the exercise need to happen as a whole group. As with everything else, it's important to be specific in your planning. You should liaise with those in leadership in your church before this session to check out the ideas on the sheet and any others you or they may have to put to the group. Stepping stones need to be built to where people actually are (not where you would like them to be). You're probably best starting with something that is low in Christian content and non-threatening. Remember that the aim is not to see people converted in one evening but to build on and strengthen an existing contact and to see folk move on. Encourage the group to think of things that may be helpful for the whole church to arrange in the third part of the exercise and pass this list on to the appropriate person. Remember that you are likely to generate more ideas than you can sensibly follow through. It will be important to discern which of the many suggestions is the appropriate first step.

The 'Stepping stones to what?' section below is important – although it need not take long. Most churches using this course will already have an *Emmaus* Nurture group in place or be planning one for the very near future. This would be a good opportunity to share the overall vision for *Emmaus* with the group.

If there are no ways people can move on in your church, then this is something you need to take up with your church leaders. Is your group called to pray for or become involved with setting up some kind of nurture group?

Stepping stones to what?

Review briefly the way people can move on in their understanding of the Christian faith in your church once they have begun to cross the stepping stones you are building.

Putting it into practice

Again, this is the most important part of the course. Remind people, that although you have finished the course, you will still be building a 'review and pray' session into regular meetings from now on.

Introduce this week's Bible readings and look ahead to whatever is coming next in the life of your group.

Summary and example timings

	mins
Buzz groups: How did it go?	20
Bible study: Witnesses and stepping stones	30
Buzz groups: Building stepping stones to faith	30
Putting it into practice	5

Building stepping stones to faith

How did it go?

Review your experience of prayer and service since you last met:

■　*Have there been any significant answers to prayer?*

■　*Have you been able to keep to the discipline of praying regularly?*

■　*Describe your experiences of serving in the way you planned last time.*

■　*Has anything happened in you or in others as a result of the serving?*

Witnesses and stepping stones

■　*Step 1 in 'Living the gospel' is to pray for your oikos.*

■　*Step 2 is to love and serve your oikos.*

■　*Step 3 is to be a witness as best you can.*

Responding to questions

Not all of us have the gift of evangelism – but we are all called to be witnesses. As we pray for people and serve people, they will begin to ask us questions.

1 Peter 3.15-16:

> But in your hearts sanctify Christ as Lord. Always be ready to make your defence to anyone who demands from you an accounting for the hope that is in you; yet do it with gentleness and reverence. Keep your conscience clear, so that, when you are maligned, those who abuse you for your good conduct in Christ may be put to shame.

Building stepping stones

Read 1 Corinthians 9.19-23.

> For though I am free with respect to all, I have made myself a slave to all, so that I might win more of them. To the Jews I became a Jew, in order to win Jews. To those under the law I became as one under the law (though I myself am not under the law) so that I might win those under the law. To those outside the law I became as one outside the law (though I am not free from God's law but am under Christ's law) so that I might win those outside the law. To the weak I became weak, so that I might win the weak. I have become all things to all people, that I might by all means save some. I do it all for the sake of the gospel, so that I may share in its blessings.

Paul's principle here is going to where people are: not just physically but spiritually. Once we have come to that point, we can build stepping stones for people as individuals and as a group.

Building stepping stones to faith

Stepping stones for individuals:

■ *Look through the list of 'individual stepping stones' on the supplementary hand-out. Put a tick by each one you think you could build for someone in your oikos.*

■ *Talk in your triplet about your finished list. Compare notes on the kinds of thing you feel able to do and to say to someone who is enquiring about faith.*

■ *Think about how you are going to serve your oikos in the coming week and pray together for the shared names.*

Stepping stones for groups

■ *Look through the list of possible stepping stones for groups to organize (you may be able to add to the suggestions here).*

■ *Think through the people you have been praying for and serving in your oikos. Which of them would come to which kind of event?*

■ *Decide on one 'stepping stone' event you can arrange as a group: set a date; begin to make plans and to pray.*

Stepping stones for churches

■ *List the stepping stones that already exist and which you can make use of as a group.*

■ *List the ways people can go further and learn more about the faith or be nurtured in faith in the life of the church.*

■ *Are there any new stepping stones that it may be helpful for the whole church to consider?*

Putting it into practice

Continue to pray for the people on your prayer list each day and for your two prayer partners.

Continue to serve your *oikos*.

Look for opportunities to build personal stepping stones.

Bible reading

About sharing faith:

John 1.35-42	Acts 8.27-40
John 2.1-11	Acts 9.10-19
John 4.1-26	Acts 19.8-12
Acts 3.1-10	Philippians 2.1-13

Building stepping stones to faith

Stepping stones

For individuals

- *Tell part of your story.*

- *Lend a book.*

- *Lend a tape.*

- *Lend a video.*

- *Help someone, e.g. take a child to cubs, parent and toddler group.*

- *Invite to a guest service.*

- *Invite to a group event.*

- *Invite to community group based on something in the news or a local issue.*

- *Share the gospel.*

Suggestions for good books, tapes and videos:

For the group

- *Open house night.*
- *Ten-pin bowling.*
- *Family fun day.*
- *Fishing trip.*
- *Christmas party.*
- *Guest nights.*
- *'Question time'.*
- *Meal together.*
- *Coach trip.*
- *Fashion evening.*
- *'Issue' evening.*
- *Sunday lunch.*
- *Men's/Women's night.*
- *Cleaning/DIY night.*

An Open House night

Guests are invited for supper and two short testimonies from group members with an invitation of how to learn more. Printed invitations say: 'Open House ... The evening will include supper and a short presentation about the Christian faith.'

Your own group's ideas:

Following on from 'Living the gospel'

In a course like 'Living the gospel', different members of your group will have learned and grasped different things – depending on where they were at the beginning.

■ *Ideally, the whole group will have moved some way in its understanding of witness and evangelism.*

■ *Some individuals will have grasped the whole idea of personal witness and will be putting it into practice.*

■ *Others will have taken just one or two things on board.*

■ *Some may have found the whole thing very difficult and will be looking forward to a much safer series of Bible studies next time round.*

Really to change the life of the group and see it become an effective base for evangelism will take more than four meetings! That's why it will be important to follow up on 'Living the gospel' over the six months that follow, in five main ways:

Through building prayer triplets into the meetings

An outline for a 15-minute review session to include in your regular meetings is given on the final optional handout. You need to get the group's agreement to follow this plan. You need to decide the frequency yourselves. Once a month may be about right, but to get into a rhythm you may want to build the review into the next four group meetings after the course ends to get people into the swing of sharing together in this way.

Through celebrating when people come to faith

It may take some time to see this begin to happen – but when it does make sure the group takes time to celebrate and rejoice in someone becoming a Christian. As members of your group's *oikos* begin to come to faith, it may be good to encourage them to come to regular group meetings before they become part of the church's nurture course. After that course finishes, they can then become members of the house group. As God continues to bless your witness as a group, that will mean that the group grows and eventually gives birth to a new group that is able to grow as well.

Alternatively, as things become more established, it may be better for the new Christian/s to remain part of the existing group, but for the foundations to be laid by going through the *Emmaus* Nurture course one to one with another group member using the handouts.

Through arranging stepping stones as a group

The initiative with this will inevitably rest with you as the leader. Try always to have one stepping stone planned, which will then act as a catalyst for the prayer, service and witness of the whole group. Different stepping stones will also bring out the gifts and interests of different group members.

Through introducing new group members to the oikos principles

That will mean working through the 'Living the gospel' material with new members as they join the group. It may be that someone else in the group could do this on your behalf (possibly in extra meetings of the prayer triplet).

Keep the vision alive

It's no small thing for a small group to engage in continuous evangelism. To sustain what is happening, you'll need to take time as a group to remember why you are doing this – it's what Jesus asks us to do!

Epilogue

A pattern for regular meetings

This is not a fifth session, but a guide for a 15-minute slot in regular group meetings (either every time you meet or as a monthly feature). The best place for it to come would be near the beginning after a time of worship and a brief introduction to the meeting's theme.

Your aim is to give an account to each other and also to encourage each other. Some of the sharing might be in the whole group and some in triplets. The prayer time could be separated from the other stages.

1   Sharing and reflection

■   *Have there been any significant answers to prayer since the last review?*

■   *Have you been able to pray; to serve; and to witness?*

2   Planning

■   *Are there particular requests for prayer in the next weeks?*

■   *Do any names need to be changed?*

■   *Any new ideas for service?*

■   *Any planning for stepping stones?*

3   Prayer

■   *For members of your oikos.*

■   *For the prayer, service and witness of the whole group.*

■   *For the forthcoming stepping stones.*

Knowing the Father

Introduction

The aim of this course is to reflect upon our experience of God and to grow in our understanding of him as our Father. There are four sessions.

Session 1 God, the Father of creation. The creative essence of God. Experience of God the Father as the loving creator. Exploring our own experience of creation and of human life.

Session 2 God, the Father of Jesus. The loving character of God. Experience of God the Father of Jesus. Looking at the person of Jesus as he reveals the Father, and the things he said about God as Father.

Session 3 God, the Father of the kingdom. The righteous purpose of God. Experience of God the Father's kingdom. Exploring our experience in the Church of trying to build the kingdom and of the work of the Holy Spirit.

Session 4 God, the Holy Trinity. This is the central doctrine of the Christian Church: our understanding of God as a community of persons – Father, Son and Holy Spirit. Exploring our experience of community and relationships.

Session One: God, the Father of creation

	mins
Group activity: Learning about each other	20
Input and discussion: How do we know God exists?	10
Buzz groups: Learning from creation	25
Input and activity: Reflecting on creation	20
Suggestions for prayer	10
Putting it into practice	5

Session Two: God, the Father of Jesus

	mins
Buzz groups: Lord, show us the Father	15
Group activity: Anyone who has seen me has seen the Father	20
Input and discussion: I am the way to the Father	10
Buzz groups: I am in the Father and the Father is in me	30
Suggestions for prayer	10
Putting it into practice	5

Session Three: God, the Father of the kingdom

	mins
Bible study and discussion: The kingdom of God	15
Input and discussion: Citizens of the kingdom	15
Buzz groups: The kingdom and the Church	25
Input and discussion: The Holy Spirit and the kingdom of God	10
Buzz groups: We praise you, O God	10
Suggestions for prayer	10
Putting it into practice	5

Session Four: God, the Holy Trinity

	mins
Buzz groups and input: Relating to the Trinity	15
Input and buzz groups: The Nicene Creed	15
Input and discussion: The story of the Trinity	25
Buzz groups: Living out the Trinity	25
Suggestions for prayer	10

God, the Father of creation

Introduction

Before the first session begins, ask all members of the group to bring with them an object that expresses something important about who they are. Not just an object that is dear to them, but something that reveals something about them.

You will probably have to contact them about this. Give a couple of examples. For instance, if you feel you are often bitter but have the potential to be lovely, bring along a jar of coffee. In the session itself, group members will share why they have brought their object as a way of showing how things can be vehicles of revelation. The coffee granules reveal something about the nature of the person.

This is done to:

■ *Break the ice at the beginning of a new set of meetings.*

■ *Find out something about each other. In presenting their object, individuals will be telling something about themselves.*

■ *Introduce the way we are going to learn during the next four sessions – beginning to understand God as Father by reflecting upon our experiences of him in different areas of life.*

Group activity: Learning about each other

Members of the group in turn show the object they have brought and explain why they have brought it. It is important to give plenty of time to this exercise – people need to get to know each other and to ask questions of each other.

Make sure you have brought an object yourself.

Input and discussion: How do we know God exists?

■ *We cannot prove or disprove the existence of God in an absolute way that will satisfy every question. As St Paul points out: 'Now we see but a poor reflection' (1 Corinthians 13.12). Only in the life to come will we see God face to face.*

■ *We can show that belief in God is reasonable. We can do this by reflecting on the things that we do know exist and that we have all experienced in one form or another. Four main areas are of particular relevance:*

   1   *We all know about our own life and our own feelings and experiences.*

   2   *We all experience the joys and wonders of the world of which we are part.*

   3   *We all know something of the story of salvation told in the Bible. Especially we know about Jesus.*

   4   *We are all members of the Church. We have experienced its life and mission. We will probably have had some experience of the Holy Spirit. We will be trying in different ways to build God's kingdom in our community.*

If God is the source of all life then, just as a beautiful painting reveals something of the nature of the painter, just as our objects revealed something about us, these things will reveal to us something of the nature of God.

Discuss in pairs how something of your own experience of these four areas has revealed to you something about God.

If there is a creation, there must be a creator.

Jesus told his disciples:

> See how the lilies of the field grow. They do not labour or spin. Yet I tell you that not even Solomon in all his splendour was dressed like one of these. If that is how God clothes the grass of the field . . . will he not much more clothe you, O you of little faith?
>
> Matthew 6.28-30

Buzz groups: Learning from creation

In this session we will be particularly looking at our experiences of life and our experiences of the world. God made the world and it is good (Genesis 1.31). He also made us in his image (Genesis 1.27).

Split into two groups and give each group a large piece of paper and some coloured marker pens. Ask one group to draw up a list of:

■ *The different things they have experienced in their lives that show that they are made by a loving Creator God.*

And the other:

■ *The different things they have experienced in the world that show the world was made by a loving Creator God.*

Encourage each group to spend time finding out why individual members find God in different things.

Now ask the groups to list on the reverse side of the paper:

■ The things they experienced in their own lives that have made belief in a loving Creator God difficult.

And the other:

■ The things they have experienced in the world that have made belief in a loving Creator God difficult.

Ask each group to make a presentation of its findings to the other. Ask them to imagine they are addressing people who are quite sceptical about God as the loving creator.

Rather than report everything they have discussed, ask them to present one thing that they think is a very good way of demonstrating God's creative love and one way they would address one of the difficult areas of experience.

So that the exercise is more than simply compiling a list, it is important to explain this clearly. You might also like to point out that 'presentation' doesn't have to mean a verbal report by one person. Some groups may want to produce a drama or draw a picture.

Explain that presentation can mean what people want it to mean!

Allow time for questions and discussion.

Input and activity: Reflecting on creation

You may want to summarize what is written in the session handout, drawing out the main points of how Christians should relate to the creation.

- *The creation reveals something of the nature of God.*

- *But the creation does not reveal everything of God's nature (only that there is a creator).*

- *We are not to worship the creation or identify God with the creation (as in some New Age beliefs).*

- *But we are stewards of the creation.*

- *And we are to delight in what God has made.*

Get groups to write a short three-line statement (something between a poem and a prayer) about God as creator of earth and heaven, and also as our Father, our creator. The lines are to begin with the letters G, O, D.

If you have a very confident group, people may want to do this as individuals. If some people are less confident, give the group the option of working in twos and threes.

Suggestions for prayer

- *A time of silence.*

- *Someone reads Psalm 8.*

- *Everyone has the opportunity to read his or her statement. Some may prefer not to, which is quite all right.*

- *Free prayer, the leader gathering together in prayer some of the concerns and issues that have arisen in the session.*

- *The Lord's Prayer and the Grace.*

Putting it into practice

Suggest that group members give some thought this week to the ways they use (or misuse) God's creation. Ask all the group members to think about any changes they might make in their lifestyle. Explain that the session next week will begin with some discussion of this.

Summary and example timings

	mins
Group activity: Learning about each other	20
Input and discussion: How do we know God exists?	10
Buzz groups: Learning from creation	25
Input and activity: Reflecting on creation	20
Suggestions for prayer	10
Putting it into practice	5

God, the Father of creation

How do we know God exists?

We cannot prove or disprove the existence of God but we can reflect upon our experience of the world and also our experience of life. If God created the world then he is also our creator. Our experience is important.

We can also show that belief in God is not unreasonable. The Church has developed certain arguments to help us here:

■   *The world has to have begun somewhere and somehow. There has to have been a 'first cause' and this first cause had to be self-sufficient and not itself caused by anything else.*

■   *The world is not random but displays design. The more recent discoveries of physics amply demonstrate the marvellous order of the universe. Many people imagine that science and scripture contradict each other. This is not so. Both describe a world of purpose and design. The Scriptures in poetic language tell us that the origin of the world is with a creator God. Human reason, and science in particular, has gone on to discover the laws that govern the universe: laws that God has put in place.*

■   *Human beings are rational and reasonable – creative, social and individual. By reflection upon our own being we are pointed beyond ourselves to a creator.*

The kernel of all these arguments is that, if there is a creation, there must be a creator.

Reflecting on creation

Reflection on creation is very important, but creation by itself cannot lead us to a full understanding of God or of life. Reflecting on the created order can lead to worshipping creation itself. The Christian view is that the world reveals something of the nature of God but we do not worship the world. Our God is both intimately involved with the world, but also separate from it.

God is also a God whose presence is revealed in human history and throughout the Scriptures. Supremely, this revelation is made known to us in Jesus Christ – God's Word made flesh. It is also prepared for in the whole history of the people of Israel to whom God makes a special revelation of himself: he is the one God and through them he will make his love known to everyone.

We can only know God completely through Jesus Christ. The creation shows us a God of order and design, but it does not show us that God loves us or has a purpose for our lives.

What is the Christian understanding of our relationship with the world?

Christians are called to be good stewards of God's creation. The world does not belong to us, it is God's. We cannot and should not do with it what we like, rather we should see that our stewardship of the world is concerned to preserve and enhance the beauty and biodiversity of creation. The Old Testament speaks about this loving care of the creation. If we take the Bible seriously then the Church will be the original Green Party!

The Old Testament speaks of a wisdom, which we would now understand as the brooding presence of the Holy Spirit, active at the dawn of creation.

> The Lord created me at the beginning of his work,
> the first of his acts of long ago.
> Ages ago I was set up,
> at the first, before the beginning of the earth.
> When there were no depths I was brought forth,
> when there were no springs abounding with water.
> Before the mountains had been shaped,
> before the hills, I was brought forth –
> when he had not ye made earth and fields,
> or the world's first bits of soil.
> When he established the heavens, I was there,
> when he drew a circle on the face of the deep,
> when he made firm the skies above
> when he established the fountains of the deep,
> when he assigned to the sea its limit,
> so that the waters might not transgress his command,
> when he marked out the foundations of the earth,
> then I was beside him, like a master worker,
> and I was daily his delight,
> rejoicing before him always,
> rejoicing in his inhabited world
> and delighting in the human race.
>
> Proverbs 8.22-31

This delight in creation is the mark of true Christian living. God has made the world and it is very good. He has made us to enjoy the world and his presence. The world is made from and filled with love. Into the world – that the beloved may know the lover – he has sent his Son.

Putting it into practice

This week think of the ways we use (or misuse) God's creation; and about any changes in lifestyle we might make as a result of our reflections.

God, the Father of Jesus

Introduction

Before the session you need to gather together as many pictures and images of Jesus as you can find – icons, devotional pictures, a madonna and child, a sacred heart, the good shepherd, etc. Ideally, find ones that not only depict different facets of his character, but also illustrate different times in his life. This might take some time, and may involve some photocopying. The effort will be worthwhile. The resource pack *The Christ We Share*, published by CMS and USPG will be very useful here. Many images of Christ are also available on the Internet.

Have them displayed in some way for people to look at as they arrive for the session.

Buzz groups: Lord, show us the Father

In the previous session, we thought about God as the Father of creation and reflected upon our experience of God as the creator of the world and as our creator. Did this make any difference to the way we have thought about the creation and the way we use it? Find out if anyone has considered this or acted upon it.

As a result of last week's reflections, a word we could use to describe God is 'creative'.

In small groups of three or four write a list of other words you would choose to describe God. At the moment, do not read the words out. We shall come back to these lists.

Group activity: Anyone who has seen me has seen the Father

Read out this short passage of Scripture. This will set the scene for the session.

> Philip said to him, 'Lord, show us the Father, and we will be satisfied.' Jesus said to him, 'Have I been with you all this time, Philip, and you still do not know me? Whoever has seen me has seen the Father. How can you say "Show us the Father"? Do you not believe that I am in the Father and the Father is in me?'
>
> John 14.8-10

This session is about our experience of Jesus as a revelation of the Father's love.

Make sure everyone has had a good look at the images on display. Ask all present to select an image that appeals to them and says something about their experience of Jesus, but ask them not to pick it up. In particular, ask people to think about Jesus showing them the Father's love. When everyone has made a choice, ask people in turn to pick up the image they have chosen and say why it appealed to them.

Afterwards put all the images back where they were.

Input and discussion: I am the way to the Father

Being able to choose is one of the vital characteristics that marks out humanity from the rest of creation. We alone are able to choose how we respond to things. We are not prisoners of instinct or environment. The one thing that can never be taken away from a person is their capacity to choose how to respond.

Someone scribbled on a wall in Auschwitz, the Nazi concentration camp: 'I believe in the sun even when it does not shine, I believe in God even when his voice is silent.'

In the same camp a Roman Catholic priest, Maximilian Kolbe, gave his own life in order to spare a fellow prisoner who, unlike him, had a wife and family.

These examples show the true dignity of humanity. They demonstrate the defeat of evil. They show that in choosing to love, even in terrible circumstances, we are children of God, made in his image.

Closely linked to the ability to choose is the ability to love. True love involves freely giving yourself to another person, if there is even a hint of coercion, it does not make it a little bit less than love, it stops being love altogether.

God wants us to enter freely into a relationship of love. Therefore he needs, at one and the same time, to demonstrate his love, but also to safeguard our freedom of choice. It is for this reason that God becomes a man. There is no other way that love can be shown and freedom of choice maintained. It is for this reason that, even in the Resurrection appearances, his identity is nearly always concealed (as on the Emmaus Road), so that even when he is risen from the dead we are not coerced into his service, but offered the invitation to love. We can choose how to respond.

This is the scandal of the gospel. Jesus does not want us as servants, he doesn't even really want us as friends. The phrase that St Paul uses is co-heirs. Jesus wants us as free lovers, blood brothers and sisters, co-heirs with him to the kingdom of heaven. And so, to show his love, he enters our world his glory veiled.

It was possible to have known Jesus all of his life on earth and never to have known his true identity as God and man. Even then it was only after his Resurrection and after the coming of the Holy Spirit that the Church was properly able to understand his identity.

Jesus is fully God and fully human. Not God disguised as a man. Not a man who is so good he is almost like God, but completely God and completely one of us. God in Jesus shares what it is to be human in order that we might share what it is to be God. Once we have entered into this relationship we discover the truth of Jesus' words to Philip. To have seen Jesus is to have seen the Father.

Read together Philippians 2.5-11 (in members' handout).

Allow time for questions and possibly some time in huddles for the group to digest this teaching.

Buzz groups: I am in the Father and the Father is in me

In the same small groups as before, write a list of words to describe the character of Jesus. Ask people to think about and share with each other their own knowledge and experience of Jesus.

Then make or draw out the following points:

■ *Often we make the mistake of applying one set of characteristics to God and another to Jesus.*

- *We should not think of Jesus as the good guy pleading to an angry God on our behalf.*

  - *Jesus is the outpouring of the Father's love.*

  - *Jesus is God come down to earth.*

  - *Jesus is God sharing human life.*

  - *Jesus is the human face of God.*

Then ask the groups to compare the two lists they have now made. How are they similar? What are the differences?

Ask the groups to draw up a definitive list of the words they would choose to describe the character of God the Father. Then get each group to report its list.

Suggestions for prayer

Give everyone a small piece of paper. From everything that has been explored this session, ask each person to write down a single word that he or she thinks describes the character of God the Father as seen through Jesus.

Ask people to look again at the images of Jesus and choose a picture that shows them the Father and which matches up with the word they have written. It doesn't matter if they choose the same image again.

If it is possible, move to another space. Around a lighted candle place the pictures and the words one by one, encouraging people to say a short prayer of thanks to the Father as they do so. Prepare for this with a time of silence.

- *Someone reads Philippians 2.5-11.*

- *The leader gathers together the thoughts and concerns of the evening in prayer.*

- *The Lord's Prayer and the Grace. In introducing the Lord's Prayer, remind everyone that when his disciples asked him how to pray Jesus began by calling God 'Our Father in heaven ...'*

Putting it into practice

Some of us have had bad experiences of earthly fathers and mothers. This week try to focus on the good qualities of parenthood shown in Jesus' revelation of the fatherhood of God. If you are a parent, can this help in your relationship with your children? We are all children. Whether our parents are alive or not; whether we liked them or not; however good or bad our relationship with them: let us give thanks and pray for them this week with God the Father's love and concern. Before going home, each person might like to reflect on this.

Summary and example timings

	mins
Buzz groups: Lord, show us the Father	15
Group activity: Anyone who has seen me ...	20
Input and discussion: I am the way to the Father	10
Buzz groups: I am in the Father ...	30
Suggestions for prayer	10
Putting it into practice	5

God, the Father of Jesus

Lord, show us the Father

How can God reveal the full nature of his love and purpose in Christ without also jeopardizing the human capacity to choose? The answer is that he is revealed to us in Jesus. That is what this session is about: God's revelation of himself in Jesus Christ. Philip says to Jesus: 'Show us the Father and that will be enough for us.' Jesus answered . . . 'Whoever who has seen me has seen the Father' (John 14.9).

Whoever has seen me has seen the Father

This passage of Scripture sets the scene for thinking about our experience of Jesus as a revelation of the Father's love.

> Philip said to him, 'Lord, show us the Father, and we will be satisfied.' Jesus said to him, 'Have I been with you all this time, Philip, and you still do not know me? Whoever has seen me has seen the Father. How can you say "Show us the Father"? Do you not believe that I am in the Father and the Father is in me?'
>
> John 14.8-10

I am the way to the Father

■ *The basis of Christian faith is relationship with God.*

■ *As Christians we believe that God has taken the initiative in this relationship by becoming a human being. The whole story of the Old Testament prepares the way for this coming of the Christ.*

■ *Therefore, if we want to know what God is like, then we must first ask what Jesus is like. Jesus is God's way to God! 'I am the way . . . to the Father' says Jesus. (John 14.6).*

St Paul wrote to the church in Philippi:

> Let the same mind be in you that was in Christ Jesus,
> who, though he was in the form of God,
> did not regard equality with God
> as something to be exploited,
> but emptied himself,
> taking the form of a slave,
> being born in human likeness.
> And being found in human form,
> he humbled himself
> and became obedient to the point of death –
> even death on a cross.

> Therefore God also highly exalted him
> and gave him the name
> that is above every name,
> so that at the name of Jesus
> every knee should bend,
> in heaven and on earth and under the earth,
> and every tongue should confess
> that Jesus Christ is Lord,
> to the glory of God the Father.
>
> Philippians 2.5-11

I am in the Father and the Father is in me

- *What do our experience of the Scriptures and our experience of Jesus reveal to us about the nature of God?*

- *What words would you use to describe God the Father as seen though the person of Jesus?*

The word Jesus used to describe God is the Aramaic word Abba, which would be best translated into English not as Father, but as Daddy. This is the intimate relationship Jesus describes. St Paul picks up the theme. When we don't know how to pray, he says, the Holy Spirit comes and prays within us, crying out – Abba, Father (Romans 8.15).

When his disciples asked Jesus to teach them to pray he began with this same familiarity born of love and trust, 'Our Father in heaven ...' (Luke 11.2).

Putting it into practice

Some of us have had bad experiences of earthly fathers and mothers. This week try and focus on the good qualities of parenthood shown in Jesus' revelation of the fatherhood of God. If you are a parent, can this help in your relationship with your children? We are all children. Whether our parents are alive or not; whether we liked them or not; however good or bad our relationship with them: let us give thanks and pray for them this week with God the Father's love and concern.

God, the Father of the kingdom

Bible study and discussion: The kingdom of God

Jesus did not come to start a new religious organization. He came to proclaim the kingdom of God. In Mark's Gospel his first words are 'The time is fulfilled, and the kingdom of God has come near; repent and believe in the good news.' What is this kingdom?

Brainstorm together to think of images and words Jesus used to describe the kingdom of God. If people are having trouble thinking of things, encourage them to spend a bit of time working in pairs looking for phrases and stories from the Bible, especially the Gospels. Looking through Matthew 13 will be particularly useful. Ideas are given on the session handout.

Write these down on a large piece of paper headed 'The kingdom of God is like . . .'

During the discussion draw out the following points:

■　*None of these images describe a geographical place.*

■　*When Jesus says the kingdom is close, he means it is available now! It is not a destination just around the corner but a new relationship with God you can enter now.*

■　*The frontiers of this kingdom run through human hearts.*

We enter the kingdom when we turn our lives around and focus on God (the true meaning of the word repent).

Input and discussion: Citizens of the kingdom

The kingdom of God is about living under the rule of God. We become citizens of the kingdom of God when we try to live by the values of the kingdom of God.

Jesus describes the qualities of this citizenship in a very famous passage in Matthew's Gospel. This is his Citizens' Charter! (For more on the Beatitudes see *Life Attitudes* by Robert Warren and Sue Mayfield.)

Read Matthew 5.3-10.

On another piece of paper headed 'Citizens of the kingdom are . . .' compile another list of words.

Now add to both lists other words or phrases from our own experience of trying to live as citizens of the kingdom of God.

If possible, display these lists where everyone can see them.

Buzz groups: The kingdom and the Church

The task of the Church is to continue the mission and ministry of Jesus: to establish God's kingdom. How, in our experience of the Church, does this actually happen? Split into two groups and address this question:

How does your church reflect the values, lifestyle and concerns of the kingdom?

Groups may need a bit of help getting into this exercise. The list of the words describing the kingdom should help. The idea is that each group examines its experience of the Church in the light of this list. So, for instance, if the kingdom of God is said to be like a priceless pearl for which we would give up everything, ask if this is the attitude we find in the Church. Or if citizens of the kingdom are supposed to be gentle, hungry for justice, pure in heart, etc., ask if these are the values manifest in the Church.

Ask each group to make a presentation of its findings under these headings:

1   Our church is close to the kingdom when . . .

2   Our church is far from the kingdom when . . .

'Presentation' means the same as it did in Session One.

Allow time for questions and discussion.

Input and discussion: The Holy Spirit and the kingdom of God

- *Through baptism we enter into a family relationship with God. Jesus is our brother and God our Father.*

- *All this happens through the activity of God the Holy Spirit.*

- *It is the Holy Spirit who makes us into the children of God.*

- *To live the life of the kingdom we need the help and power of the Holy Spirit.*

That is why, when Jesus commissioned his Church to continue his ministry, he first gave them the Holy Spirit (see John 20.21-22).

- The more we live in this way, the closer we shall come to knowing God, the Father of the kingdom.

Buzz groups: We praise you, O God

Split into groups of three and ask each group to write a short three-line prayer of thanksgiving about its understanding of God based on what has been explored in the sessions so far. Therefore it is to include:

- *One line about God's creativity, which we explored in Session One.*

- *One line about God's loving character, which we explored in Session Two.*

- *One line about God's purpose, which we have looked at in this session by exploring what we mean by God's kingdom.*

Suggestions for prayer

The different statements are read out. As they were written in groups of three, you could ask each member to read out one line.

The leader reads one of the parables of the kingdom from Matthew 13. This really needs to be decided on the night so as to reflect the interests and enthusiasms of the session.

The leader gathers together some of the concerns of the session in prayer.

The Lord's Prayer and the Grace.

Putting it into practice

God has a purpose for the world and for every human life. If living in his kingdom is about living under his law, then what are the marks of a Christian lifestyle? How should citizens of the kingdom be different from other people?

Think and pray about this. Come ready next week to share any conclusion you have come to or decisions you have made.

Make sure the statements about God are collected together, as they will be needed in the next session.

Summary and example timings

	mins
Bible study and discussion: The kingdom of God	15
Input and discussion: Citizens of the kingdom	15
Buzz groups: The kingdom and the Church	25
Input and discussion: The Holy Spirit and the kingdom of God	10
Buzz groups: We praise you, O God	10
Suggestions for prayer	10
Putting it into practice	5

God, the Father of the kingdom

The kingdom of God

Through baptism we enter into a family relationship with God and the Holy Spirit commissions us to help build God's kingdom. The Bible tells the story of God's relationship with the world, his action in creation and in human history. Its major theme is the rule of God.

By pondering on what it means to live under the rule of God and to work to establish the kingdom of God, we can discover a lot about the nature of God, particularly his purpose for the world.

Jesus uses many images to describe what the kingdom of God is like. Which ones speak powerfully to you? What do they tell you about the purpose and nature of God?

Here are some ideas from the Scriptures.

The kingdom of God is like . . .

- *A man sowing seed in a field (Matthew 13.18-23).*

- *A mustard seed itself (Matthew 13.31-32).*

- *A portion of yeast (Matthew 13.33).*

- *Treasure hidden in a field (Matthew 13.44).*

- *A merchant looking for fine pearls (Matthew 13.45-46).*

- *A dragnet cast into the sea (Matthew 13.47-50).*

What are your ideas?

Citizens of the kingdom

Jesus describes the qualities of this citizenship in a very famous passage in Matthew's Gospel. This is his Citizens' Charter! It speaks of the attitudes we are called to have and the blessings we will receive.

> Blessed are the poor in spirit, for theirs is the kingdom of heaven.
> Blessed are those who mourn, for they will be comforted.
> Blessed are the meek, for they will inherit the earth.
> Blessed are those who hunger and thirst for righteousness, for they will be filled.
> Blessed are the merciful, for they will receive mercy.
> Blessed are the pure in heart, for they will see God.
> Blessed are the peacemakers, for they will be called children of God.
> Blessed are those who are persecuted for righteousness' sake, for theirs is the kingdom of heaven.
>
> *Matthew 5.3-10*

What does your experience of being part of the Church tell you about the work of the Holy Spirit guiding people into this way of living?

The kingdom and the Church

Membership of the Church is not like joining another organization. It is initiation into a new way of living.

The task of the Church is to continue the mission and ministry of Jesus: to establish God's kingdom. How, in your experience of the Church, does this actually happen?

How does your church reflect the values, lifestyle and concerns of the kingdom?

Putting it into practice

Think and pray about the marks of a Christian lifestyle. How should citizens of God's kingdom be different from other people?

Come next week ready to share any conclusion you have come to or decisions you have made.

God, the Holy Trinity

Introduction

In this session you will be referring to the Nicene Creed, which is printed in the supplementary handout, and the Icon of the Trinity (also called The Hospitality of Abraham) by Andrej Rublev. This famous icon is easily obtained from a Christian bookshop, or from the Internet, and you may want to make a copy for each member of the group. You will also need the statements about the nature of God that were prepared in the last session.

St Paul's Multimedia publications, who produce a range of Christian pictures in different sizes, also do a copy of Rublev's Icon of the Trinity. Their address is: St Paul Multimedia Productions, 133 Corporation Street, Middle Green, Slough, SL3 6BS.

Buzz groups and input: Relating to the Trinity

Put people in the same groups of three that they were in at the end of the last session, when they wrote their three-line statement about God. Hand out the statements.

Ask people to share together how they relate to different persons in the Trinity. Be sensitive here. Give people 'permission' to express how they relate to God (not how they think they should relate).

Then get them to note the Trinitarian structure of the statement they prepared. One line was about God's creativity. This refers to God the Father. One was about God's loving character. This refers to God the Son. One was about God's purpose. This refers to God the Holy Spirit. But they are all about God. Father, Son and Holy Spirit are all creative, all loving, all filled with righteous purpose, but we experience these different aspects of the one God through the experience of three persons.

A simple way of trying to understand is to think about the one substance H_2O, and the three manifestations – water, ice and steam. You may even want to prepare a demonstration of this by having on display a glass of water, an ice cube and a boiling kettle giving off steam.

Input and buzz groups: The Nicene Creed

Remind people that it is in the name of God, the Holy Trinity that we were all baptized. The earliest creeds of the Church were a set of questions asked before baptism: do you believe in God the Father, God the Son and God the Holy Spirit?

Staying in the same small groups, ask people to look at the Nicene Creed (in the supplementary handout) and to note its Trinitarian structure. Which sections refer to the Father, which to the Son and which to the Holy Spirit?

If you want to, you could also look at the questions asked of candidates in baptism and confirmation. If there are recently baptized and confirmed people in the group, they will remember these three-fold questions, which summarize the whole Christian faith.

Input and discussion: The story of the Trinity

This section is also a summary of all that has been explored in this course.

You may want to draw a simple visual aid as you talk, writing down on a large piece of paper the words Father, Son, Holy Spirit.

- *The understanding of God as Holy Trinity developed in the Church by reflection upon experience. That is why we have been finding out about God in this course by reflecting upon our experience of him.*

- *The earliest Christians were all Jews. Therefore they believed in one God, who was the source of everything. We explored these ideas in Session One.*

- *Jesus presented a problem. After God had raised him from death, they experienced him as their Lord and Saviour. Did that mean there were two gods? Or was Jesus somehow always part of what it had always meant to believe in one God? We explored these ideas in Session Two.*

- *The Holy Spirit also presented a problem. They experienced the Holy Spirit as the life and power of Jesus coming from the Father. Were there three gods? Or was the Holy Spirit part of what it had always meant to believe in one God? We explored some of these ideas in Session Three.*

- *Belief in the Trinity, as it came to be known several hundred years later, is revelation – the experience of Jesus and the Holy Spirit – and reflection upon experience – the continual process whereby the Church (that's us!) reflects upon the meaning of the gospel and the significance of Jesus.*

- *The Trinity is about our belief in God. It safeguards the belief that Jesus is fully human and fully God. It is the central belief of the Christian Church.*

Allow as much time as the group needs for questions and discussion around these points.

Buzz groups: Living out the Trinity

At the end of last week's session, we asked what difference being a Christian might make to our lifestyle.

What did people come up with?

Allow time for some general discussion.

Our understanding of God as Trinity suggests these ideas about living the Christian life. Split into groups for further discussion:

1   God is understood to be a community of persons – three persons, distinct and individual, but one in creativity, love and purpose. This understanding of God could be a model for human society. How should human communities reflect the Trinitarian community of God?

2   One of the best ways of understanding the Trinity is by seeing how the Father, Son and Holy Spirit are in a perfect relationship of love with one another. This understanding of God could be a model for human relationships. How should human relationships reflect the Trinitarian relationship of God?

These questions may seem complicated. It is really a matter of reflecting upon experience. What have been our best experiences of human community? Was it not when men and women were treated as equal and shown decency, love and respect? What have been our best experiences of human relationships? Was it not when sacrifice, trust and unconditional love were shown?

In saying this, we are only acknowledging that we cannot begin to know how to be human until we have begun to know God the source of humanity. The doctrine of the Trinity reveals that God is a community of persons in a relationship of self-giving love.

This resonates with the insights of contemporary psychology and sociology. True humanity can only be found in relationship with others. True community can only be found when we live in harmony and justice. All this comes from God who is community and relationship.

After discussion in the groups, allow time for general discussion and questions.

Finish by asking each member of the group to say briefly whether thinking about God as Trinity, in the way this course has developed, will make a difference to any aspect of their Christian life. Allow a short time of silence to prepare.

Suggestions for prayer

Prepare a place for prayer and light three candles, one for each person of the Trinity. You will be referring to Rublev's Icon of the Trinity. The extract from Robert Warren's book given in the supplementary handout can be used as an introduction to the icon as you prepare to lead the prayer time, or used as an additional handout.

Have some gentle music playing.

Lead a meditation upon the icon.

■ *Invite people to look at it in silence. There is a sense in which the image is incomplete. It seems there is a place for a fourth person. That person is each one of us. God invites us to join his community of love.*

■ *Invite people to place themselves in the picture and to bring to God their needs: especially to live in community and to have godly relationships.*

■ *Point out the cup placed on the table. Consider the Eucharist (Holy Communion) as the meal of the kingdom of God, where we are invited to sit at table in the banquet of heaven.*

■ *Ask people to give thanks for their experiences of community and of good relationships.*

End with the Lord's Prayer and the Grace.

Summary and example timings

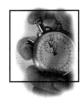

	mins
Buzz groups and input: Relating to the Trinity	15
Input and buzz groups: The Nicene Creed	15
Input and discussion: The story of the Trinity	25
Buzz groups: Living out the Trinity	25
Suggestions for prayer	10

God, the Holy Trinity

Relating to the Trinity

The Christian faith understands God as Father, Son and Holy Spirit.

> Righteous Father,
> the world does not know you, but I know you;
> and these know that you have sent me.
> I made your name known to them,
> and I will make it known,
> so that the love with which you have loved me
> may be in them, and I in them.
>
> John 17.25-26

These verses get to the heart of what it means to believe in God as Holy Trinity. Jesus came to the world to make God known. He reveals to a lost world that the God who created them is also their Father who loves them. He promises that the love that is in the Father and the Son will also be in those who follow the one, true God. The Holy Spirit coming from the Father and the Son will make a home in all who believe and trust. Thus, when we become Christians, at our baptism we are asked whether we believe and trust not just in Jesus, but in Father, Son and Holy Spirit – the God of love who is a community of love and who lives in a loving, creative relationship.

The Nicene Creed

Some Christians say the Nicene Creed in the Eucharist every Sunday (see supplementary handout). It encapsulates all we believe about God. Its structure is an expansion of the three questions we were asked at our baptism:

■   *Do you believe and trust in God the Father?*

■   *Do you believe and trust in God the Son?*

■   *Do you believe and trust in God the Holy Spirit?*

To recite the creed is not just to read out a list of things we believe in, but also to describe a relationship we trust in.

The story of the Trinity

The Trinity is the central belief of the Christian Church. It developed in the Church as Christians reflected upon their experience of God, of Jesus and of the Holy Spirit. It safeguards our belief that Jesus is fully human and fully divine. By describing God as a community it also enriches the community of our life on earth and invites us into relationship with God.

This is the real significance and glory of knowing God as Trinity. We are invited to share this relationship of love. Human life is drawn into the life of God.

Living out the Trinity

Our understanding of God as Trinity suggests ideas about living the Christian life.

1   God is understood to be a community of persons – three persons, distinct and individual, but one in creativity, love and purpose. This understanding of God could be a model for human society. How should human communities reflect the Trinitarian community of God?

2   One of the best ways of understanding the Trinity is by seeing how the Father, Son and Holy Spirit are in a perfect relationship of love with one another. This understanding of God could be a model for human relationships. How should human relationships reflect the Trinitarian relationship of God?

God, the Holy Trinity

The Nicene Creed

We believe in one God,
the Father, the Almighty,
maker of heaven and earth,
of all that is,
seen and unseen.

We believe in one Lord, Jesus Christ,
the only Son of God,
eternally begotten of the Father,
God from God, Light from Light,
true God from true God,
begotten, not made,
of one Being with the Father;
through him all things were made.
For us and for our salvation he came down from heaven,
was incarnate from the Holy Spirit and the Virgin Mary
and was made man.
For our sake he was crucified under Pontius Pilate;
he suffered death and was buried.
On the third day he rose again
in accordance with the Scriptures;
he ascended into heaven
and is seated at the right hand of the Father.
He will come again in glory to judge the living and the dead,
and his kingdom will have no end.

We believe in the Holy Spirit,
the Lord, the giver of life,
who proceeds from the Father and the Son,
who with the Father and the Son is worshipped and glorified,
who has spoken through the prophets.
We believe in one holy catholic and apostolic Church.
We acknowledge one baptism for the forgiveness of sins.
We look for the resurrection of the dead,
and the life of the world to come. Amen.

From *Common Worship, Services and Prayers for the Church of England*, 2000

God, the Holy Trinity

Rublev's icon

The icon represents the story of the three visitors whom Abraham and Sarah had when they 'entertained angels unawares' (Genesis 18). Those visitors came to tell them that they would have a son within the year – at which news Sarah laughed.

Orthodox spirituality sees in those visitors a picture of the Trinity. Rublev represents them sitting before a table with a chalice on it (remember Abraham went and killed an animal for the meal). On the right-hand side is a figure clothed in green and blue robes. Those robes represent the green of earth and the blue of heaven. It is the figure of the Holy Spirit. He is both the One who comes from heaven (blue) as the communicator of divinity to humanity, and yet also the One at home on earth (green), for he was the agent of creation when the world was made, and when the Son was conceived (Genesis 1.2 and Luke 1.35). He is the One who introduces us to the Godhead.

In this icon, the figure representing the Holy Spirit has his head bowed towards the person in the centre, robed partly in blue and partly in the royal robes of empire. This is the figure of Jesus. The One who, in a unique way came from heaven, but who now has returned to glory as the all-conquering king who overcame through death, defeating evil by the power of unselfish, sacrificial and forgiving love. His head is also bowed as he looks to the figure on the left of the picture.

This third figure is robed in translucent robes that speak of an inner glory which shines for ever. Here the Father is seated in majesty, yet also as the one who visits this earth. Remember '*God* was reconciling the world to himself in Christ' (2 Corinthians 5.19, author's italics).

These figures are seated in a circle, but it is not a completed or closed circle. It is a 'C' not an 'O'. The whole picture invites us in – to complete the circle, to be part of the life of mutual love, affirmation and creativity which characterise the interaction within the Trinity. What an immense and incredible privilege. This is the source of vitality for all living. No wonder we can simply stand before such a presence and, without a word, enter in through the door of adoration.

From Robert Warren, *An Affair of the Heart*, 1994, pp. 40–41

Knowing Jesus

Introduction

Rather than try to deal with the whole span of Jesus' life and ministry, this module aims to answer some basic questions:

- *Who is Jesus?*

- *What was his teaching?*

- *What did he do?*

- *What difference does he make?*

New Christians need to deal with these questions not only for their own growth, but in order to be equipped to witness to the reality of Christ in the world. This course takes us into the realm of some fundamental Christian doctrines – in particular the Incarnation (how Jesus is both divine and human) and the Atonement (how Jesus' death reconciles us with God).

In looking at some of these fundamental questions about Jesus, we shall be starting from the Bible. Plenty of biblical references have been given, but it will not always be necessary or helpful to look these up in the group. It is easy to swamp people with texts so that they are not able to see the wood for the trees. However, leaders need to be familiar with the passages in order to be able to draw on them as appropriate.

Although beginning with the New Testament, this module cannot remain there. The Church's understanding of who Jesus is and what he accomplished came into sharper focus as it addressed the heresies and controversies that led eventually to the formulating of the creeds in the fourth and fifth centuries. Led by the Holy Spirit, successive generations of Christians, under the authority of Scripture and guided by Christian understanding down the ages, have to answer these fundamental questions about Jesus in order to present the gospel afresh to their contemporaries. In doing so they will be influenced by their context.

Thus thinking about the cross, in the twentieth century, took place in the context of two world wars and, in particular, the holocaust. This has led to an emphasis on the suffering of God as seen in the writings of theologians like Jürgen Moltmann, who sees the cross as the event of God's love in which the Son suffers abandonment by the Father, the Father suffers the death of the Son, and the Holy Spirit is the powerful love that spans the gulf between Father and Son and so reaches godforsaken humanity. It is important that leaders take seriously the questions raised by group members, because many of these will arise out of their context and life experience. For the gospel of Jesus to be good news, it must be able to hear and address these questions.

Nor can we leave our study of Jesus simply at the level of our thinking and understanding. In the Gospels, Jesus calls people to follow him: to become his disciples. The course ends with a look at being a disciple of Jesus today and what that means for us.

Sessions One and Three contain activities using visual images of Jesus and of the cross. It may be helpful to begin gathering this material immediately in order to have as wide a selection as possible. Visits to the art section of the local library, with reference to contemporary as well as classical artists, may prove fruitful but so may posters from Christian bookshops, and borrowing crosses and other objects, with permission, from local churches and downloading images from the Internet. Two useful resources available from Church Mission Society, Partnership House, 157 Waterloo Road, London SE1 8UU are *The Christ We Share* and *A-cross the World* – both contain good visual images. The National Gallery also produces a resource pack for schools with reproductions of famous paintings depicting the life of Christ.

The suggested linkwork (Putting it into practice) for this module is the consecutive reading of the Gospel of either Luke or John – letting the text speak for itself. If your group is made of up relatively new Christians, you might like to direct them to Luke's Gospel, as John's offers a more theological interpretation of who Jesus is. If the group has recently completed the *Emmaus Nurture* course, members may have read Luke as part of that. However, do not be overly directive, as people will be more motivated to read if they have been given the choice. The Bible Society produces some very attractive modern language versions of the Gospels. It might be worth having copies of these available for group members to buy. They are convenient to carry and can be marked as people read them in a way some are hesitant to do with their full Bibles. Alternatively, people may prefer to listen to a tape or CD, which may be purchased from Christian bookshops or the Bible Society.

Further reading

Books about Jesus abound. Two scholarly but accessible books for leaders who want some serious background reading would be *The Meaning of Jesus* by N. T. Wright and M. J. Borg, SPCK 1999 and *The Mystery of Salvation*, The Church of England Doctrine Commission, Church House Publishing, 1995.

Session One: Who is Jesus?

	mins
Buzz groups and discussion: Who do you say that I am?	15
Input: What the Church believes about Jesus	10
Bible study and discussion: Jesus is fully human	15
Buzz groups: What would it mean to . . .?	10
Bible study and discussion: Jesus is fully divine	15
Buzz groups: How would you answer . . .?	10
Prayer together	10
Putting it into practice	5

Session Two: What did Jesus teach?

	mins
Buzz groups: The teaching of Jesus in a nutshell	10
Input and discussion: The kingdom of God	20
Bible study: The parables of the kingdom	15
Buzz groups: Write your own parable	15
Input and discussion: Signs of the kingdom	15
Prayer together	10
Putting it into practice and preparation for Session Three	5

Session Three: Why did Jesus die?

	mins
Group activity: Looking at the cross	10
Bible study and discussion: Why the cross?	5
Group activity: At the foot of the cross	25
Input and discussion: The meaning of the cross	20
Buzz groups: The cross is central to our worship	15
Prayer together	10
Putting it into practice	5

Session Four: The difference Jesus makes

	mins
Group activity: A postcard to a friend	10
Input and discussion: Why Jesus is important	20
Group activity: A resolution to learn more	10
Bible study and discussion: How should we respond to Jesus?	20
Buzz groups: A challenge to discipleship	15
Prayer together	10
Putting it into practice	5

Who is Jesus?

Buzz groups and discussion: Who do you say that I am?

In Matthew 16.13-17 we read that Jesus asked his disciples two questions: Who do people say I am? Who do you say I am? These are the questions we will begin to address during this module. We will look together at what the Bible says about Jesus, about what the Church has said about him and explore our own experience of him.

If a group of people is talking about Jesus, we might presume that each was talking about the same person. This is not necessarily so! Even within the Church people have different pictures and images of Jesus, different views of who he is and why he is important. So let's begin by thinking about our own views.

Choose either Exercise 1 or 2. The first is better, if you can get hold of the pack.

Exercise 1

Spread out the pictures of Jesus from *The Christ We Share* and invite group members to choose the one that appeals to them most. (These packs are available to buy from Church Mission Society but also to borrow from many diocesan resource centres.) When each person has chosen, invite individuals to say why they chose their particular picture. Using the list in Exercise 2, talk about some of the ways in which people who are not Christians think about Jesus.

Exercise 2

Either in small buzz groups or as one group, ask people to share how their picture and understanding of Jesus have changed over the years. Why have their views changed?

It might be helpful to ask people to think of the picture they had of Jesus as a child, as a teenager, before they became a Christian (if their journey to faith has been as an adult) and now. If you have asked people to share in small groups, use a time of plenary discussion to draw out some of the pictures.

Ideally, the sharing will touch on some incomplete or less than helpful views of Jesus. It may help to list on a large piece of paper some of the ones the group comes up with. Here are some possibilities (but don't go through them all with the group):

- *'Gentle Jesus meek and mild' who was there to bless when needed but never challenged views or made demands.*

- *A good moral teacher.*

- *A distant figure who lived in a world of stained glass windows.*

- *A historical figure who may have been a spiritual teacher but quite unlike the claims the Church has made for him.*

- *An 'existentialist' Jesus who becomes whatever people need him to be, someone about whom there are no absolutes.*

- *A New Age Jesus, a spiritual guru who embodied the spark of divine life in everyone.*

- *A Jesus about whom we can know almost nothing because the records can't be trusted.*

- *A Jesus of popular literature and cinema. Different portrayals have suggested a fraudulent Jesus, a confused Jesus, a tempted and sinning Jesus, a magical Jesus. The possibilities are almost endless!*

After the introductory exercise, look together at Mark 8.27-33. Notice the answers the disciples give to the two questions.

1   People were interpreting who Jesus was in the light of their own experience. John the Baptist was a popular religious leader who had recently been killed; Jews believed that Elijah would return to herald the age of the Messiah, the dawn of the kingdom of God; one of the prophets; i.e. they recognized that he was a religious teacher and leader of significance.

2   Peter says that Jesus is the Messiah, God's specially chosen and anointed agent. In Matthew's Gospel, Jesus says to Peter that flesh and blood did not reveal this to him, it is an insight that comes from God himself. Jesus then goes on to teach the disciples about his suffering, his death and his Resurrection. In doing this, he is affirming the truth of Peter's statement but beginning to reinterpret the disciples' understanding of what it meant to be the Messiah.

If we are to grow in our understanding of who Jesus is, then we need the help of our own and other people's experience as brought to us in Scripture and the teachings of the Church, but we also need the inspiration and insight that come from God's Holy Spirit. This would be a good point to stop for a moment and *pray* for the course.

Input: What the Church believes about Jesus

As you run through the story of the Church's understanding about Jesus, it may help to construct a simple visual aid. Borrow a child's jigsaw puzzle (the kind with very large pieces), which you assemble on the floor picture side down, or alternatively make your own out of thick cardboard. Tape labels or write on the pieces to correspond to the different pieces of the jigsaw that led to the creeds. Then assemble the pieces as you are talking.

Alternatively, paste a large poster of Jesus on to card, then cut it up jigsaw style and write the different parts of the evidence in felt pen over the top of the picture. Again, assemble the picture as you are talking.

Jesus' words	Jesus' actions	Jesus' death and Resurrection
The experience of the disciples	The teaching of the New Testament	The teaching of the Church fathers

The pieces should read: Jesus' words; Jesus' actions; Jesus' death and Resurrection; the experience of the disciples; the teaching of the New Testament, and the teaching of the Church fathers.

The Church's understanding of who Jesus is and what he has done did not happen overnight. Rather like doing a jigsaw puzzle, the whole picture began to emerge as different pieces fell into place. First of all there is the evidence of what Jesus himself did and said; then there is the evidence of his death and Resurrection; add to that the experience of the disciples in the months and years that followed, the insights of Paul and the other New Testament writers and then the insights gained as the Church fathers, the leaders of the Church in the first five centuries, defended the faith, as they had come to understand it, against heretical attacks, and we get eventually to the statements about Jesus in the historic creeds. Refer to the section about Jesus in the Nicene Creed. (The full text is in the supplementary handout 1 for Session Four of 'Knowing the Father'; you may like to copy this and give it out for your group.)

In other words, the Church came to affirm that Jesus was uniquely both fully human and fully God. In this session we are going to look at both these aspects of his person, beginning with his humanity.

Bible study and discussion: Jesus is fully human

What evidence is there from the Gospels that Jesus was fully human?

Ask people not to look at their handouts for a few minutes while you draw out from them some of the following. Ask the group what evidence there is that Jesus was fully human. You could write the answers on a large sheet of paper on the floor. Alternatively, you could continue the 'puzzle' theme, with different members of the group putting in different pieces and reading aloud the verses, which could be written on the back. The full list of points and Bible references is in the members' handout.

Ask the group why it is important that Jesus was fully human?

In discussion draw out the following:

- *He appreciates what it is like to be human; he understands us (Hebrews 4.15-16).*

- *It is central to the salvation he accomplished for us. (More of this in Session Three.)*

- *As the only perfect human being, he offers us an example to follow.*

Buzz groups: What would it mean to …?

Ask people to spend a few minutes in groups discussing what it would mean to the following people that Jesus was fully human:

- *someone recently bereaved*

- *someone unjustly accused*

- *someone made redundant.*

You could split into three groups and ask each group to discuss one scenario.

Bible study and discussion: Jesus is fully divine

Despite his evident humanity, it became clear to the disciples that Jesus was more than simply a man. The evidence is cumulative. You could either ask the group what evidence it can think of and make a list or, again, continue the jigsaw theme by giving out pieces containing the points in the members' handout. You will need to be selective about which verses from the handout are read out. Those who are interested can look up the rest of the evidence later.

Summary

The doctrine of the Incarnation is the teaching of the Church that says God became man in Jesus Christ. The significance of this is summed up by Dorothy L. Sayers: 'If Christ were only man, then he is entirely irrelevant to any thought about God; if he is only God, then he is entirely irrelevant to any experience of human life.'

C. S. Lewis wrote to his friend Arthur Greaves on 11 December 1944: 'The doctrine of Christ's divinity seems to me not something stuck on which you can unstick but something which peeps out at every point so that you'd have to unravel the whole web to get rid of it.'

For C. S. Lewis, the coherence of Christianity was such that it was impossible to eliminate the idea of the divinity of Christ without doing such damage to the web of Christian doctrine that the entire structure of the Christian faith would collapse.

Buzz groups: How would you answer . . .?

Either:

Split into smaller groups and answer the question: How would you answer a critic of Christianity who said that 'Jesus was just a good man' or 'Jesus is just one of the world's great religious teachers. He is no more important than Mohammed or the Buddha?'

Or:

The creeds were written to defend Christianity against particular heresies. What are the truths about Jesus that we most need to defend/proclaim today? Split into smaller groups and write a brief creed for the contemporary world.

Prayer together

You might like to light a candle and put around it the pictures of Jesus chosen by group members in the first exercise. Alternatively, you could put out some objects to represent Jesus' humanity and divinity (e.g. a crib from a nativity set, a cross or crucifix, an icon of the Resurrection, some vine leaves and grapes). Ask someone to read the quotation below from John Blanchard.

> Nobody knows the exact date of his birth, but that one event divides the whole of world history into the years labelled BC and AD.
>
> He never wrote a book, but more books have been written about him than about anyone else in history. The nearest thing we have to his biography – the part of the Bible called the New Testament – has been translated in whole or in part into about 1,500 languages.
>
> He never painted a picture or composed any poetry or music, but nobody's life and teaching has been the subject of a greater output of songs, plays, poetry, pictures, films, videos and other art forms.
>
> He never raised an army, but millions of people have laid down their lives in his cause. It has been calculated that every year the almost unbelievable number of 330,000 of his followers are martyred for their faith.
>
> John Blanchard, *Will the Real Jesus Please Stand Up*,
> Evangelical Press, 1989. Used with permission.

In Matthew 1.21 and 23 we read of two of the names given to Jesus before his birth – Jesus (God saves) and Emmanuel (God with us).

Invite people to spend a few moments in quietness thinking about which is the more important for them right now.

Of course, both are equally important because they show us different aspects of the person and work of Jesus. Other names used of him in the New Testament also tell us something about him. In an attitude of reflection and worship, invite people to mention names of Jesus that are important to them. Ask them to, as it were, drop the names into the silence.

You might like to end by singing a traditional hymn like 'How sweet the name of Jesus sounds' or a worship song like 'Jesus, name above all names'.

Putting it into practice

Putting it into practice for this module is very straightforward. If we are to grow in our appreciation of Jesus, then we need to learn as much about him as possible. The Gospels were written not only to tell us the story of Jesus, but also that we might come to appreciate his significance. They do this in different ways. Luke sets out, as he says at the beginning of his Gospel, 'to write an orderly account' for Theophilus, who may have been a Roman Christian or, because his name means 'lover of God', may simply represent the new Christian who has recently been taught about the faith. John's Gospel states clearly, 'Jesus did many other signs in the presence of his disciples, which are not written in this book. But these are written so that you may come to believe that Jesus is the Messiah, the Son of God, and that through believing you may have life in his name' (John 20.30-31).

The group has the choice of reading either Luke's account of Jesus or John's or listening to them on a tape or CD. If different members of the group choose different Gospels, that will not matter. Indeed, it will help to bring a variety of insights into the group. Ask members to try to set aside time early in the week to read or listen to the chapters at one sitting. This way they will get a better overview. They can always go back later in the week to think about particular passages that interest, inspire or puzzle them.

This week's passages are Luke 1.1 – 6.49 or John 1.1 – 5.47.

Summary and example timings

	mins
Buzz groups and discussion: Who do you say that I am?	15
Input: What the Church believes about Jesus	10
Bible study and discussion: Jesus is fully human	15
Buzz groups: What would it mean to . . .?	10
Bible study and discussion: Jesus is fully divine	15
Buzz groups: How would you answer . . .?	10
Prayer together	10
Putting it into practice	5

Who is Jesus?

Who do you say that I am?

> When Jesus came into the district of Caesarea Philippi, he asked his disciples, 'Who do people say that the Son of Man is?' And they said, 'Some say John the Baptist, but others Elijah, and still others Jeremiah or one of the prophets.' He said to them, 'But who do you say that I am?' Simon Peter answered, 'You are the Messiah, the Son of the living God.' And Jesus answered him, 'Blessed are you, Simon son of Jonah! For flesh and blood has not revealed this to you, but my Father in heaven.
>
> Matthew 16.13-17

Notice the answers the disciples give to the two questions.

1   People were interpreting who Jesus was in the light of their own experience.

2   Peter says that Jesus is the Messiah, God's specially chosen and anointed agent. In Matthew's Gospel, Jesus tells Peter that flesh and blood did not reveal this to him, it is an insight from God himself.

To grow in our understanding of who Jesus is, we need to reflect on our own experience and that of other people as brought to us in the Bible and the teachings of the Church, but we will also need the inspiration and insight that come from God's Holy Spirit.

What the Church believes about Jesus

The Church's understanding of who Jesus is and what he has done did not happen overnight. Like a jigsaw puzzle, the whole picture began to emerge as different pieces fell into place.

First there is the evidence of what Jesus himself did and said; then the evidence of his death and Resurrection; add to that the experience of the disciples in the time that followed and then the insights gained as the Church fathers, the leaders of the Church in the first five centuries, defended the faith against heretical attacks, and we eventually reach the statements about Jesus in the historic creeds.

The Church came to affirm that Jesus was uniquely both fully human and fully God.

Jesus is fully human

■   *He was born from the womb of a woman (Luke 2.5-7) and acknowledged Mary as his mother.*

■   *He is given a human lineage (Matthew 1.1-16; Luke 3.23-38).*

■   *He grew and developed physically, emotionally, spiritually (Luke 2.40,52).*

■   *He ate food (Luke 7.34; 14.1), experienced hunger and thirst (Luke 4.2), tiredness (John 4.6) and needed to sleep (Matthew 8.24).*

■   *He was limited by time and space (John 11.17).*

- *He felt human emotions: love (Mark 10.21), grief (Matthew 14.12-13; John 11.35), compassion (Mark 1.41; 6.34), anger (Mark 3.5; 10.14), surprise (Matthew 8.10; Mark 6.6).*

- *He built relationships with disciples and friends (John 11.35-36; 15.15).*

- *He was dependent upon God and spent time in prayer (Mark 1.35; Luke 6.12).*

- *He suffered mental and physical pain (Luke 22.43-44; Mark 15.15-20).*

- *He died (Mark 15.37).*

This is backed up by the rest of the New Testament e.g. Romans 1.3; 9.5, Galatians 4.4, 1 Timothy 2.5, Hebrews 2.14, 1 John 4.2.

The New Testament makes it clear that Jesus was like us in every way, but without sin (Hebrews 4.15-16).

Jesus is fully divine

1 Evidence from his ministry

- *He taught and healed with authority (Mark 1.22, 40-42).*

- *He claimed the right to forgive sins (Mark 2.3-12; Luke 7.36-50).*

- *He exercised power and authority over nature (Matthew 8.23-27; 14.23-33).*

- *The demons recognized him (Matthew 8.28; Mark 1.24).*

- *He claimed superiority over divinely given laws and institutions like the Sabbath (Luke 6.5).*

- *He called God Father and himself Son, indicating an equality and reciprocity in his relationship with God (Matthew 11.25-27; John 5.19-23; 10.14-30).*

- *According to the Gospels he spoke of himself in terms that might be interpreted as implying divinity, and acknowledged this when others implied it (Matthew 14.33; 16.16; 26.63-65; the 'I am' sayings of John's Gospel).*

- *He was acknowledged 'Son of God' in his baptism and transfiguration (Matthew 3.17; 17.5).*

- *The signs of the virginal conception and Resurrection affirm and confirm his divinity.*

2 The witness of the Early Church

- *They proclaimed and worshipped him as Lord, a title usually reserved for God (Acts 2.36; Philippians 2.5-11; Romans 10.13).*

- *John's Gospel teaches clearly that he is God (John 1.1-4, 14, 18; 14.6, 7; 20.28).*

- *He is regarded as creator of the universe, and saviour of his Church (Colossians 1.16-17; Hebrews 1.1-2).*

- *Jesus uniquely reveals what God is like (Hebrews 1.3; Colossians 1.15).*

3 The Church came to believe that no other explanation did justice to who Jesus really is.

Putting it into practice

Choose to read or listen to either Luke's or John's account of Jesus from beginning to end. To give you a better overview, try to set aside time early in the week to study the chapters at one sitting.

This week's passages are Luke 1.1 – 6.49 or John 1.1 – 5.47.

What did Jesus teach?

Introduction

In preparation for this session it may be helpful to read Session Three 'God, the Father of the kingdom' from 'Knowing the Father', the second course in this book.

Buzz groups: The teaching of Jesus in a nutshell

Allow people a few moments to share any reflections or questions arising from Session One or Putting it into practice.

In pairs, write down one sentence that you think summarizes Jesus' teaching. Read the sentence to the rest of the group.

Input and discussion: The kingdom of God

Have either a sheet of flipchart paper and write on it as you go or prepare separate pieces of paper beforehand and put them down as you come to each point.

> Jesus came to Galilee, proclaiming the good news of God, and saying, 'The time is fulfilled, and the kingdom of God has come near; repent, and believe in the good news.'
>
> Mark 1.14,15

For Mark, the message of Jesus can be summarized as good news of the kingdom of God. Let's look at what that means:

■ *The Jewish people had been looking forward to the kingdom of God for hundreds of years. It would be a time when God would rule as king, a time of justice and peace when God's enemies would be overthrown and his people would be set free. (In popular Jewish thought the kingdom took several different forms – political and apocalyptic.)*

If you are using a large piece of paper, write down: **The kingdom of God – foretold in the Scriptures.**

■ *In Jesus the kingdom has dawned. Read Luke 4.16-21.*

Write: **Fulfilled in Jesus**

■ *The kingdom is demonstrated in the actions of Jesus, healing the sick, exorcising the demonized, befriending the outcast and the sinner – the kingdom was good news of deliverance. (Matthew 11.2-6)*

Write: **Demonstrated**

■ *The kingdom is inclusive not exclusive, especially of the poor and the marginalized. Jesus spent time with and had a special care for those whom the religious people of his day despised, e.g. women and children, tax collectors, prostitutes, lepers. (Mark 2.13-17)*

Write: **Inclusive**

■ *The kingdom is hidden and growing. (Matthew 13.31-33)*

Write: **Grows in secret**

■ *The kingdom demands a response. (Matthew 13.44-45)*

Write: **Demands a response**

■ *The values of the kingdom are different from those of the world (the Sermon on the Mount in Matthew 5 – 7 and especially 5.3-13; 6.19-34; 7.21-27).*

Write: **Different values**

■ *The kingdom is both present in Jesus and coming in all its fullness when Jesus returns. (Matthew 25.31-46)*

Write: **Now and not yet**

■ *The kingdom is not about a place, it is about the rule of God in people's lives and in his world.*

Write: **Where God reigns**

When we become Christians, we become citizens of the kingdom of heaven because we acknowledge God's rule in our hearts and our lives. The welcome in the Anglican service of baptism in *Common Worship* puts it like this:

> We welcome you into the fellowship of faith;
> we are children of the same heavenly Father;
> we welcome you.

What practical difference should it make to our lives that we are citizens of the kingdom of heaven? Can you think of examples of Christians, either today or in history, whose faith has had a radical impact on their priorities and lifestyle?

(Recent examples might be people like Desmond Tutu or Mother Teresa of Calcutta or Martin Luther King, historical ones might be people like Lord Shaftesbury or John Newton or Elizabeth Fry.)

Bible study: The parables of the kingdom

Much of Jesus' teaching was given in the form of parables: stories with a meaning. Originally they spoke specifically into Jesus' historical and religious context. They were part of Jesus' challenging of the status quo, of his proclamation of the dawning of the kingdom of God. However, the parables also speak to us. They tell us things (a) about God, (b) about our response to the kingdom.

Divide a large piece of paper into two columns and write 'About God' and 'Our response' at the top of each column. Ask the group for examples of parables they can remember and try to place them under one of the columns. Draw out from the group members what they think each parable is about. Looking through Bibles for ideas is allowed. Don't worry if some parables don't fit or could go in both columns!

The following may help you to prompt the group if people get stuck but begin with their ideas.

Parables about the nature of God

The parable of the lost sheep in Luke 15.1-7 emphasizes that he is a God of grace who takes the initiative in looking for and restoring the lost. The other two parables in that chapter, the lost coin (Luke 15.8-10) and the lost son (Luke 15.11-32) make the same point. The extent of God's generosity is emphasized in the parable of the workers in the vineyard (Matthew 20.1-16).

Parables about the kind of response expected from those who belong to the kingdom

The parable of the pharisee and the tax collector (Luke 18.9-14) emphasizes the need to recognize our own sinfulness if we are to enter the kingdom. The importance of recognizing our sinfulness and need of change is also a theme in the parable of the lost son. The parable of the talents (Matthew 25.14-30) encourages us to use our God-given gifts, while the parable of the ten virgins (Matthew 25.1-13) and the waiting servants (Luke 12.35-40) speak of the importance of keeping alert and watchful. The parables of the hidden treasure and the fine pearl (Matthew 13.44-45) remind us that God's kingdom is worth sacrificing everything for. Other parables speak about the way we should relate to and care for other people, e.g. the unforgiving servant (Matthew 18.21-35); the good Samaritan (Luke 10.25-37); the sheep and goats (Matthew 25.31-46); and the rich man and Lazarus (Luke16.19-31). The kingdom of God is about justice and righteousness, a whole new way of living that puts loving our neighbour second in importance only to loving God (Matthew 22.39).

Buzz groups: Write your own parable

Much of Jesus' teaching was built around ordinary events and experiences that people of his day could relate to – like sheep, agriculture and servants. In doing so, he helped them understand that God comes to us and wants to speak to us in our everyday lives. If he were teaching today, he might use supermarkets, motorways and the Internet. In small groups try to create a parable showing some aspect of the kingdom of God, using a feature of contemporary society. Remember that most of Jesus' parables were short and had one main point, so keep it simple. Share your stories with one another.

Input and discussion: Signs of the kingdom

Jesus' actions reinforced his teaching. John's Gospel calls the miracles 'signs' because they point beyond themselves to Jesus and his kingdom. On one occasion (you may have mentioned it earlier) John the Baptist sends messengers to Jesus to ask whether he was indeed the Messiah come to inaugurate God's kingdom. Jesus says to them, 'Go back and report to John what you hear and see: the blind receive sight, the lame walk, those who have leprosy are cured, the deaf hear, the dead are raised, and the good news is preached to the poor.' (Matthew 11.4-5; Luke 7.22)

We have already seen how Jesus' miracles often involved those who were the outcasts of society – the lepers, a centurion, a woman with a haemorrhage, a blind beggar, a Syro-Phoenician woman, a madman who lived among the tombs because everyone was afraid of him. He was demonstrating to people the unconditional love of God and the scope of the kingdom as a place of welcome for all.

He often commended people for their faith (Mark 5.34; 10.52; Luke 17.19). It is through faith or trust in God and his Son Jesus that we enter the kingdom of God and share its benefits.

When Jesus sent his disciples out to teach and proclaim the kingdom of God, he gave them power and authority to heal the sick and cast out demons (Luke 9.1-6; 10.1-9). In what ways is the Church today called to demonstrate the kingdom?

Prayer together

The following prayers come from the Iona Community. You might like to use one or both. The responses to each are printed on the handout for the session.

You broke down the barriers when you crept in beside us.
For in Jesus ... the smiling Jesus,
    the story-telling Jesus,
    the controversial Jesus,
    the annoying Jesus,
    the loving and forgiving Jesus,
your hands touched all, and touched us,
showing us that in Christ
there is neither Jew nor Gentile,
    neither male nor female:
All: All are one in Jesus Christ
and for this we praise you.

You opened our eyes
to see how the hands of the rich were empty
and the hearts of the poor were full.
You dared to take the widow's mite,
    the child's loaves
    the babe at the breast,
and in these simple things
to point out the path to your kingdom.
You said 'Follow me!',
for on our own we could never discover
that in Christ
there is neither Jew nor Gentile,
    neither male nor female:
All: All are one in Jesus Christ,
and for this we praise you.

You gave us hands to hold:
black hands and white hands,
African hands and Asian hands,
the clasping hands of lovers,
and the reluctant hands of those
who don't believe they are worth holding.
And when we wanted to shake our fist,
you still wanted to hold our hand,
because in Christ
there is neither Jew nor Gentile,
    neither male nor female:
All: All are one in Jesus Christ,
and for this we praise you.

Here in the company
of the neighbour whom we know,
and the stranger in our midst,
and the self from whom we turn,
we ask to love as Jesus loved.
Make this the time and the place, good Lord,
when heaven and earth merge into one,
and we in word and flesh can grasp
that in Christ
there is neither Jew nor Gentile
    neither male nor female:
**All: All are one in Jesus Christ,
and for this we praise you.
Amen.**

Lord God,
In Jesus, you came in the body:
flesh of our flesh, bone of our bone,
one with us in searing pain and delirious laughter.
We thank you that you did not remain an idea,
    even a religious idea,
But walked, wept and washed feet among us.

By your love,
change our ideas, especially our religious ideas,
into living signs of your worth and will.
**All: Through our lives and by our prayers,
your kingdom come.**

Lord God,
In Jesus, you touched the suffering,
    listened to the ignored,
    gave the depressed something to hope for.
You bandaged the broken with love
and you healed them.
We believe that your power to heal is still present, so on your help we call.
We remember those whose minds are menaced by thoughts which worry or wound them,
(pause)
we remember those whose hearts are broken because love has gone, or because the light
they lived by has turned to darkness, (pause)
we remember those whose feet walk in circles, stopping only when they are tired, resting
only to walk in circles again, (pause)
we remember those whose flesh and bone or mind and spirit are filled with pain, (pause)
we remember those who feel discarded or disposable. (pause)

O Christ, put your hands where our prayers beckon.
**All: Through our lives and by our prayers,
your kingdom come.**

Lord God,
in Jesus your body was broken
by the cowardly and the powerful.
The judgement hall of Pilate knew your silence as surely as your critics
knew your voice.
In word and in silence,
take on the powerful of the world today:
those whose word sentences some to cruelty or unmerited redundancy;
those whose word transfers wealth or weapons for the sake of profit or
prejudice;
those whose silence condones the injustice they have the power to change.

O Saviour of the poor, liberate your people.
**All: Through our lives and by our prayers,
your kingdom come.**

Lord God,
by the authority of scripture,
we learn that we are the body of Christ . . .
Yes, even we who worship in different ways,
     even we whose understanding of you is so changeable,
     even we who, in our low moments,
     make an idol of our insignificance.
We are your body, we are told.

Then, Lord,
make us like you,
that our souls may be the stained glass
through which your light and purpose
bring beauty and meaning to the world.
**All: Through our lives and by our prayers,
your kingdom come.**

Your kingdom come
in joy and generosity,
in the small and the large, the ordinary and the special,
and to you be the glory
now and always.
Amen.

From *A Wee Worship Book*, Wild Goose Worship Group

Many of the hymns and songs from the Wild Goose Resource Group of the Iona Community speak of the kingdom of God. Perhaps you could play something from one of their CDs or sing something like 'Seek ye first the kingdom of God' or 'The kingdom of God is justice and joy'.

Putting it into practice and preparation for Session Three

This week's passages are Luke 7.1 – 12.59 or John 6.1 – 12.50.

Ask members of the group to bring to the next session any pictures of the cross or crosses or crucifixes that are important to them.

Summary and example timings

	mins
Buzz groups: The teaching of Jesus in a nutshell	10
Input and discussion: The kingdom of God	20
Bible study: The parables of the kingdom	15
Buzz groups: Write your own parable	15
Input and discussion: Signs of the kingdom	15
Prayer together	10
Putting it into practice and preparation for Session Three	5

What did Jesus teach?

The kingdom of God

> Jesus came to Galilee, proclaiming the good news of God, and saying, 'The time is fulfilled, and the kingdom of God has come near; repent and believe in the good news.'
>
> Mark 1.14,15

The message of Jesus can be summarized as good news of the kingdom of God.

■   *The Jewish people had been looking forward to the kingdom of God for hundreds of years. It would be a time when God would rule as king, a time of justice and peace when God's enemies would be overthrown and his people would be set free.*

■   *In Jesus the kingdom had dawned (Luke 4.16-21).*

■   *The kingdom was demonstrated in the actions of Jesus (Matthew 11.2-6).*

■   *The kingdom was inclusive not exclusive (Mark 2.13-17).*

■   *The kingdom is hidden and growing (Matthew 13.31-33)*

■   *The kingdom demands a response (Matthew 13.44-45).*

■   *The values of the kingdom are different from those of the world (the Sermon on the Mount in Matthew 5 – 7 and especially 5.3-13; 6.19-34; 7.21-27).*

■   *The kingdom is both present in Jesus and coming in the future in all its fullness when Jesus returns (Matthew 25.31-46).*

■   *The kingdom is not about a place, it is about the rule of God in people's lives and in his world.*

When we become Christians, we become citizens of the kingdom of heaven, because we acknowledge God's rule in our hearts and our lives.

The parables of the kingdom

Much of Jesus' teaching was given in the form of parables: stories with a meaning. They spoke specifically into Jesus' context and were part of his challenging the status quo and his proclamation of the kingdom of God. They speak to us today about God and about our response to the kingdom.

The main groups of parables are about the nature of God and the kind of response expected from those who belong to the kingdom. Jesus built them around ordinary events and experiences that people of his day could relate to – like sheep, agriculture and servants. In doing so he helped them understand that God comes to us and wants to speak to us in our everyday lives. If he were teaching today, he might use supermarkets and motorways and the Internet.

Signs of the kingdom

Jesus' actions reinforced his teaching. John's gospel calls the miracles 'signs' because they point beyond themselves to Jesus and his kingdom. On one occasion John the Baptist sends messengers to Jesus to ask whether he was indeed the Messiah come to inaugurate God's kingdom. Jesus says to them:

> Go and tell John what you hear and see: the blind receive their sight, the lame walk, the lepers are cleansed, the deaf hear, the dead are raised, and the poor have good news preached to them.
>
> Matthew 11.4-5

Jesus' miracles often involved those who were the outcasts of society – the lepers, a centurion, a woman with a haemorrhage, a blind beggar, a Syro-Phoenician woman, a madman who lived among the tombs because everyone was afraid of him. He was demonstrating to people the unconditional love of God and the scope of the kingdom as a place of welcome for all.

He often commended people for their faith (Mark 5.34; 10.52; Luke 17.19). It is through faith or trust in God and his son Jesus that we enter the kingdom of God and share its benefits.

When Jesus sent his disciples out to teach and proclaim the kingdom of God, he gave them power and authority to heal the sick and cast out demons:

> Then Jesus called the twelve together and gave them power and authority over all demons and to cure diseases, and he sent them out to proclaim the kingdom of God and to heal.
>
> Luke 9.1-2

In what ways is the Church today called to demonstrate the kingdom?

Prayer together

The following responses in prayers from the Iona Community may be used:

All: All are one in Jesus Christ,

and for this we praise you.

All: Through our lives and by our prayers,

your kingdom come.

Putting it into practice and preparation for Session Three

This week's passages are Luke 7.1 – 12.59 or John 6.1 – 12.50.

Please bring to the next session any pictures of the cross or crosses/crucifixes that are important to you.

Why did Jesus die?

Group activity: Looking at the cross

The cross is central to Christianity. Just as we will never understand all there is to know about God, so we will never understand all there is to know about the cross – when all has been said and done, it remains a profound mystery. However, it is important to try to think about why the cross is so important and explore some of its many facets.

Invite group members to share the different portrayals of the cross they have brought with them: pictures, crucifixes, crosses, etc. You might add some of your own. (There are some particularly striking pictures of the crucifixion by third world artists in *The Christ We Share*.) Look at them as a group and discuss the different messages they convey.

Input and discussion: Why the cross?

This section could be omitted depending upon how long you allow for the film clip in the next section.

Historically, the crucifixion can be understood as the response of the religious and political authorities to what they saw as the provocation of Jesus' words and actions. However, from the earliest times, Christians believed that the cross was necessary. It was part of God's plan and not an awful mistake. Many, though not all, scholars think that Jesus himself believed his messianic task of bringing in the kingdom of God would be accomplished through his own suffering and death.

In Luke's account of the resurrection appearance to the two disciples on the road to Emmaus (Luke 24.13-27), Jesus explains that it was necessary for him to suffer.

> He said to them, 'Oh, how foolish you are, and how slow of heart to believe all that the prophets have declared! Was it not necessary that the Messiah should suffer these things and then enter into his glory?' Then beginning with Moses and all the prophets, he interpreted to them the things about himself in all the scriptures.
>
> Luke 24.25-28

Group activity: At the foot of the cross

Either watch a video/DVD of Jesus' trial and crucifixion (Zeffirelli's *Jesus of Nazareth* or an extract from Mel Gibson's *The Passion of the Christ* remain reasonably faithful to the biblical text) or read together a dramatized account of the Passion narrative and Resurrection from *The Dramatised Bible*, Lent, Holy Week and Easter or from pre-prepared photocopied sheets from one of the Gospels, giving different members different parts.

(Some of the group may well have watched the Zeffirelli video as part of the *Emmaus* Nurture course – if so, make sure you do something different at this point.)

Watching a portrayal of the crucifixion always has an emotional as well as a spiritual impact.

Great sensitivity is needed on the part of the group leader at this point. Leaving a few minutes' quiet for personal reflection may be important before moving into sharing and discussion. Prayer thanking Jesus for the cross and asking that we might understand it more fully might also be appropriate.

When you feel it right to move on, put a large piece of paper on the floor and ask people to suggest words that, for them, summarize what the cross is all about. Write them on the paper.

Input and discussion: The meaning of the cross

Have you noticed how Paul never really mentions anything about Jesus' earthly life except his death and Resurrection? Have you noticed too how these nearly always go together? (1 Corinthians 15.1-7; Philippians 3.10-11; Romans 6.3-5) The resurrection was God's affirmation or 'yes' to Jesus' self-offering on the cross. It is our assurance that all that Jesus died to accomplish is complete. It is God's sign of hope for individuals and the world. When we speak about the cross of Christ, we do not focus narrowly on his crucifixion, but on all that is involved in his suffering, his death, his Resurrection and his Ascension.

In 1 Corinthians 15.3 Paul says, 'For I handed on to you as of first importance what I in turn had received: that Christ died for our sins in accordance with the scriptures' – but what does that mean? Is that all there is to the cross? The New Testament uses different images or pictures to try to help us understand the meaning of the cross. Some of them are easier for us to understand today than others. None is a complete explanation in itself. The meaning of the cross is always greater than the sum total of the different pictures. It is rather like looking at a very precious cut jewel. At any one time we may concentrate on one particular facet. In doing so we may not be able to focus clearly on the other facets, but they are always there and it is the jewel itself that is valuable, not just one aspect of it.

Here are some of the facets of the jewel of the cross. At different times in the history of the Church, some have seemed more prominent or important than others. The same will be true for individuals. There will be times in our lives when one aspect of the cross speaks to us more strongly than another. (In working through these different aspects of the cross, try to relate them to the words on your piece of paper.)

As you talk, create a very simple visual aid with the cross at the centre and five strings or ribbons going out from it. As you cover each aspect of the meaning of the cross, place a card or piece of paper with the key word at the end.

■   *On the cross Jesus identified with our human predicament and took our place.*
     (Keyword: **Identification**)*

     In his life Jesus identified with suffering humanity. He healed the sick, befriended the outcast, freed the oppressed and forgave sinners. He ended up where any of these could have ended up: a failure, condemned as a criminal, in agonizing pain, deserted by his friends, forsaken by God. But he did this not because he deserved it, but because he freely chose to share our failure, condemnation, despair and godforsakenness. And in so doing he brings the love of God into the depths where God's absence is known. Because he suffers the absence of God, no one else need do so.

■   *As the friend betrayed, Jesus deals with all that destroys relationships and offers restoration and reconciliation. (Keyword:* **Reconciliation**)*

     At the Eucharist (Holy Communion) Christians say 'in the same night that he was betrayed ...' This is not simply a way of dating the Last Supper nor of reminding us of something Judas did. It reminds us that the story of God's dealings with the human race is one of repeated betrayal. Like the parable of the tenants in the vineyard, the coming of Jesus is the climax of all those times when God comes and is rejected by his people. In the cross we see the extent of God's faithfulness and constant love in the face of human rejection. But the cross is about more than

God's love and faithfulness: the New Testament teaches that, through the cross, we are 'put right with God', our relationship with him is restored. Paul also teaches that, because of the cross, barriers between individuals and groups are broken down and relationships restored.

■ *In the cross Jesus triumphs over all the powers of sin and evil. (Keyword: **Victory**)*

Colossians 2.15 says Jesus 'disarmed the rulers and authorities and made a public example of them, triumphing over them in it [the cross].' Because of the death and Resurrection of Jesus, sin and death and evil can no longer have a final hold over us. As Paul says in Romans 8.31-39, nothing can now separate us from the love of God in Christ Jesus our Lord.

■ *In the cross Jesus identifies with all the pain and suffering in the world. (Keyword: **Suffering**)*

'If there is a God of love, why does he allow so much suffering?' is a question asked from time to time by Christians as well as unbelievers. There are no easy answers. Some suffering is clearly the result of human sin but much is not. Because of the cross, we can say that God does not stand aloof from the suffering of his world but enters into it in the person of Jesus, who suffered not just physically but mentally, emotionally and spiritually.

The only ultimately satisfactory response to the problem of unmerited or disproportionate suffering is to believe that our creator, through a wonderful act – at once of self-limitation and self-expression, is present in the darkest affliction, shares our pain, bears our sorrows, and sustains us through it all, creating good in spite of evil, so revealing the true nature of divine power as showing mercy and pity.

The Mystery of Salvation, p.113.

Or as Shillito's poem 'Jesus of the Scars' puts it:

The other gods were strong but Thou wast weak;
They rode but Thou didst stagger to thy throne.
Yet to our wounds only God's wounds can speak
And not a god hast wounds but Thou alone.

From William Temple, *Readings in St John's Gospel*

■ *On the cross Jesus shows us perfect love. (Keyword: **Love**)*

Not only is the cross the supreme demonstration of God's love for us (John 3.16), it shows us how we ought to live our lives in response to that love.

Buzz groups: The cross is central to our worship

Choose either (a) or (b)

(a) The Eucharist (Holy Communion)

The Eucharist or service of Holy Communion is the most important service in many churches. Central to this service is the remembering of Christ's self-giving love on the cross. At the Last Supper Jesus said, 'Do this in remembrance of me.' Either take the Eucharistic prayer used in your church or use the one from *Common Worship* on the supplementary handout. Ask the group which aspects of the cross are remembered and celebrated in it. Are there any missing? Are there any themes that have not been mentioned so far?

(b) Hymns and songs

Different aspects of Christ's work on the cross are reflected in the hymns we sing. Give each member of the group a copy of a hymn or song book that you use in church. Invite them to look at a selection of hymns or songs about the cross – you will probably need to give them a starter list of about ten and then leave the group to suggest others (which may or may not be in the book).

Ask the group what aspects of the cross are picked up in the different hymns. Invite each person to select which one most nearly expressed what they want to say about the cross.

Some suggestions are:

When I survey the wondrous cross

We sing the praise of him who died

Man of Sorrows! what a name

Come and see, come and see, come and see the King of love

Meekness and majesty

My Lord, what love is this that pays so dearly

He was pierced for our transgressions

Hail, thou once despised Jesus

The price is paid; come, let us enter in

And can it be that I should gain

Christ the Lord is risen again!

Prayer together

Place a simple cross or a selection of the pictures used at the beginning of the session in the centre of the room as a focus for your prayers. Philippians 2.5-11 would be a good passage to read. Either invite members of the group to pray simple prayers of response to the love of God shown to us in the death and Resurrection of Jesus, or use some you have prepared in advance. If you have chosen the hymn option, you might like to sing one or two that most nearly expressed what the group wanted to say about the cross.

Putting it into practice

The passages for this week are Luke 13.1 – 19.44 or John 13.1 – 17.26.

Summary and example timings

	mins
Group activity: Looking at the cross	10
Bible study and discussion: Why the cross?	5
Group activity: At the foot of the cross	25
Input and discussion: The meaning of the cross	20
Buzz groups: The cross is central to our worship	15
Prayer together	10
Putting it into practice	5

(NB timings in this session will vary depending upon which film/dramatic reading is chosen. Considerably longer may be needed for 'At the foot of the cross'.)

Why did Jesus die?

Looking at the cross

The cross is central to Christianity. Just as we will never understand all there is to know about God, so we will never understand all there is to know about the cross – when all has been said and done, it remains a profound mystery. However, it is important to try to think about why the cross is so important and explore some of its many facets.

The Gospels encourage us to see the cross as part of God's plan and not an awful mistake. In Luke's account of the resurrection appearance to the two disciples on the road to Emmaus (Luke 24.13-27), Jesus explains that it was necessary for him to suffer.

> He said to them, 'Oh, how foolish you are, and how slow of heart to believe all that the prophets have declared! Was it not necessary that the Messiah should suffer these things and then enter into his glory?' Then beginning with Moses and all the prophets, he interpreted to them the things about himself in all the scriptures.
>
> Luke 24.25-28

The meaning of the cross

Have you noticed how Paul never really mentions anything about Jesus except his death and Resurrection? Have you noticed too how these nearly always go together? (1 Corinthians 15.1-7; Philippians 3.10-11; Romans 6.3-5) The Resurrection was God's affirmation or 'yes' to Jesus' self-offering on the cross. It is our assurance that all that Jesus died to accomplish is complete. It is God's sign of hope for individuals and the world. When we speak about the cross of Christ we do not focus narrowly on his crucifixion but on all that is involved in his suffering, his death, his Resurrection and his Ascension.

In 1 Corinthians 15.3 Paul says, 'For I handed on to you as of first importance what I in turn had received: that Christ died for our sins in accordance with the scriptures' but what does that mean? Is that all there is to the cross? The New Testament uses different images or pictures to try to help us understand the meaning of the cross. The meaning of the cross is always greater than the sum total of the different pictures. It is rather like looking at a very precious cut jewel. At any one time we may concentrate on one particular facet. In doing so we may not be able to focus clearly on the other facets but they are always there and it is the jewel itself that is valuable, not just one aspect of it.

Here are some of the facets of the jewel of the cross. At different times in the history of the Church, some have seemed more prominent or important than others. The same will be true for individuals. There will be times in our lives when one aspect of the cross speaks to us more strongly than another.

■ **Identification** *On the cross Jesus identified with our human predicament, suffering and sin and took our place. He freely chose to share our failure, condemnation, despair and godforsakenness.*

- **Reconciliation** As the friend betrayed, Jesus deals with all that destroys relationships and offers restoration and reconciliation between individuals and God and between different people.

- **Victory** In the cross, Jesus triumphs over all the powers of sin and death and evil.

- **Suffering** In the cross, Jesus identifies with all the pain and suffering in the world.

- **Love** On the cross, Jesus shows us how much God loves us and sets us an example of perfect love.

Putting it into practice

The passages for this week are Luke 13.1 – 19.44 or John 13.1 – 17.26.

Why did Jesus die?

You are worthy of our thanks and praise,
Lord God of truth,
for by the breath of your mouth
you have spoken your word,
and all things have come into being.

You fashioned us in your image
and placed us in the garden of your delight.
Though we chose the path of rebellion
you would not abandon your own.

Again and again you drew us into your covenant of grace.
You gave your people the law and taught us by your prophets
to look for your reign of justice, mercy and peace.

As we watch for the signs of your kingdom on earth,
we echo the song of the angels in heaven,
evermore praising you and *saying*: Holy, holy, holy . . .

Lord God, you are the most holy one,
enthroned in splendour and light,
yet in the coming of your Son Jesus Christ
you reveal the power of your love
made perfect in our human weakness.

Embracing our humanity,
Jesus showed us the way of salvation;
loving us to the end,
he gave himself to death for us;
dying for his own,
he set us free from the bonds of sin,
that we might rise and reign with him in glory.

On the night he gave up himself for us all
he took bread and gave you thanks;
he broke it and gave it to his disciples, saying:
Take, eat; this is my body which is given for you;
do this in remembrance of me.

In the same way, after supper
he took the cup and gave you thanks;
he gave it to them, saying:
Drink this, all of you; this is my blood of the new covenant
which is shed for you and for many for the forgiveness of sins.
Do this, as often as you drink it, in remembrance of me.

Therefore we proclaim the death that he suffered on the cross,
we celebrate his resurrection, his bursting from the tomb,
we rejoice that he reigns at your right hand on high
and we long for his coming in glory.

As we recall the one, perfect sacrifice of our redemption,
Father, by your Holy Spirit let these gifts of your creation
be to us the body and blood of our Lord Jesus Christ;
form us into the likeness of Christ
and make us a perfect offering in your sight.

Look with favour on your people
and in your mercy hear the cry of our hearts.
Bless the earth,
heal the sick,
let the oppressed go free
and fill your Church with power from on high.

Gather your people from the ends of the earth
to feast with [N and] all your saints
at the table in your kingdom,
where the new creation is brought to perfection
in Jesus Christ our Lord;

by whom, and with whom, and in whom,
in the unity of the Holy Spirit
all honour and glory be yours, almighty Father,
for ever and ever. **Amen.**

Eucharistic Prayer F from *Common Worship* © The Archbishops' Council, 2000

The difference Jesus makes

If you are using the handout, it is best not to give it out until after the first group activity.

Group activity: A postcard to a friend

Last session we thought about the meaning of the cross as being at the heart of what Jesus came to do. But the death of Jesus is not the starting-point for the Christian faith. The starting-point is the Resurrection. If Jesus had not been raised from the dead then, as Paul says in 1 Corinthians 15.14, our faith is in vain. It was the experience and conviction of the disciples that God had raised Jesus from the dead that helped them to understand the significance of his death.

Those who have taken part in the *Emmaus* Nurture course will already have had an opportunity to examine the evidence for the Resurrection. What we are really concerned with in this session are the fruits of the Resurrection.

The evidence for the Resurrection begins with the experience of the first disciples. Time and again they encountered the risen Christ when they were least expecting him. It is one of the most distinctive features of the Resurrection accounts in the Gospels that, every time the risen Jesus appears in their midst, the disciples are surprised, afraid or doubting. Those who say that the Resurrection was a figment of the disciples' imagination, a wish fulfilment, are simply not looking at the evidence! This evidence was reinforced by the fact of the empty tomb, the fact that so many people encountered the risen Christ (1 Corinthians 15.3-8 as well as the Gospels) and that this encounter transformed their lives to such a degree that they were prepared to bear public witness to the reality of the Resurrection in the face of persecution, imprisonment and death (Acts 4.1-12,19-20,33; 10.39-41; 17.17-18).

Before his death, Jesus promised his disciples that he would send the Holy Spirit to be with them for ever, that he would help them to understand more about Jesus and to bear witness to him. After his Resurrection, Jesus told the disciples to wait in Jerusalem until they had received power from on high to enable them to be his witnesses (Acts 1.4-5, 8; 2.1-12,22-24,36-39). It has been the testimony of Christians down the ages that, through the working of the Holy Spirit, they meet with the risen Lord Jesus and he makes a difference to their lives.

Before looking further at the difference Jesus makes, we are going to reflect on our own experience of him.

Give everyone a postcard and something to write with. Ask them to write a postcard to a friend saying as simply and concisely as possible the difference Jesus has made to their lives.

Allow a maximum of five minutes for this, then ask people to read out what they have written. You might like to summarize some of the differences that Jesus makes on a large piece of paper so that you can refer to it in what follows.

Input and discussion: Why Jesus is important

This section is best approached flexibly. Build on the sharing that has just taken place. You might like to begin by highlighting those things on the list about which people have already spoken and then move on to discuss things that were not raised by the postcards. Give people time to ask questions and to share their experiences. Where you think it will be helpful, encourage the group to look up the Bible passages to reflect on them in the light of experience, but don't feel bound to look up too many – people can do that at home! Give out the handout if you have not already done so.

- *Jesus shows us what God is like and makes it possible for us to know the Father.*

  John 1.18; John 14.6-10,20-21; Colossians 1.15-20; Hebrews 1.3;

- *Jesus makes it possible for us to be forgiven and make a new start.*

  Acts 2.38; Romans 6.3-11; 2 Corinthians 5.17-21; 1 John 1.6 – 2.2;

- *Jesus has conquered death and promises us that we shall be raised.*

  John 11.25-26; 1 Corinthians 15.20-26; 1 Thessalonians 4.13-14;

- *Jesus has promised us the gift of the Holy Spirit.*

  John 7.37-39; Acts 1.4-8; Acts 2.33,38-39; Romans 8.14-16,26-27;

- *Jesus promises to be with us at all times and in all circumstances.*

  Matthew 28.18-20; John 14.18-23; Romans 8.35-39;

- *Jesus shows us what it is like to be truly human and live life to the full. He received life as a gift from the Father and demonstrated what it is to be dependent on him. He showed that it is possible to live a holy life, a life dedicated to God, while at the same time enjoying people and parties, appreciating creation, and not being bound by human conventions and laws.* John 10.10;

- *Jesus incorporates us into a new family, the Church.*

  Luke 8.19-21; Galatians 4.4-7; Ephesians 3.14-19; 1 Peter 2.9-10;

- *Jesus has broken down the walls that divide individuals and communities.*

  Galatians 3.27-29; Ephesians 2.8-22;

- *Jesus has taught us how to pray and still prays for us.*

  Matthew 6.5-15; Luke 11.1-13; Hebrews 7.25;

- *Jesus feeds and sustains us in our Christian journey.*

  Matthew 11.28-30; John 6.35-40; John 15.4-11;

- *Jesus is Lord of heaven and earth.*

  Philippians 2.5-11; Matthew 28.19-20.

Group activity: A resolution to learn more

Ask people to turn their cards over and write a second note. This will say what aspects of who Jesus is and what he does they hope to learn more about in the next few months. Invite people to read these out to the group.

Bible study and discussion: How should we respond to Jesus?

In this course we have thought about who Jesus is, what he taught and did while on earth, what he has done through his death and Resurrection and why he is important. In the light of all this, how should we respond?

Read Luke 1.26-38.

Mary was a very ordinary person, a young girl from a humble background. She was confused and frightened by the angel's appearance and greeting. She did not really understand all that God was inviting her to be part of, but everything that she knew of God up to that point encouraged her to trust him. 'I am the Lord's servant . . . May it be to me as you have said' (Luke 1.38). She said yes to God. She did not understand fully what this would mean. She pondered on her experiences (Luke 2.19,51). She learned to trust her son Jesus and encouraged others to do so too (John 2.5). She was there at his crucifixion (John 19.25-27) and, although we do not know whether Jesus appeared to her after his Resurrection, she was there with the disciples in the upper room praying for the coming of the Holy Spirit (Acts 1.14).

For many Christians throughout the centuries Mary has been the model of discipleship, someone who responded to God in loving, trusting obedience. As a result of her 'yes' Christ was born in her. Her role, as the mother of our Lord, was unique. But Paul assures us that Jesus lives in all who put their trust in him (Galatians 2.20; Colossians 1.27). We too are invited to be Christ-bearers. It is as we say yes to God day by day and trust in all that Jesus has done for us, that the life of Jesus is shaped and formed in us as individuals and as his body, the Church. We are able to share him with a needy world.

Buzz groups: A challenge to discipleship

People who encountered Jesus in the Gospels were given an invitation to come and follow and to become a disciple. A disciple is a lifelong learner. But the word also implies wholehearted commitment to Jesus and his ways: a leaving behind as well as a following.

Read the call of the first disciples in Mark 1.14-20.

Does Jesus still call us to this leaving and wholehearted commitment today?

Does he call every Christian to this total discipleship – or just some people?

Read aloud *The Fellowship of the Unashamed* below. How do people respond to that measure of commitment?

I am part of the 'Fellowship of the Unashamed'. I have Holy Spirit power. The die has been cast. I've stepped over the line. The decision has been made. I'm a disciple of His. I won't look back. I won't look back, let up, slow down, back away or be still. My past is redeemed, my present makes sense, and my future is secure. I am finished and done with low living, sight walking, small planning, smooth knees, colourless dreams, tame visions, mundane talking, chintzy giving and dwarfed goals!
I no longer need pre-eminence, prosperity, position, promotions, plaudits or popularity.
I don't have to be right, tops, recognised, praised, regarded or rewarded. I now live by presence, learn by faith, love by patience, live by prayer and labour by power.

My face is set, my gait is fast, my goal is heaven, my road is narrow, my way is rough, my companions few, my guide reliable, my mission clear. I cannot be bought, compromised, detoured, lured away, turned back, diluted or delayed. I will not flinch in the face of sacrifice, hesitate in the presence of adversity, negotiate at the table of the enemy, ponder at the pool of popularity or meander in the maze of mediocrity.
I won't give up, shut up, let go or slow up until I've preached up, prayed up, paid up, stored up and stayed up for the sake of Christ.

I am a disciple of Jesus. I must go till He comes, give till I drop, preach till all know and work till He stops.

And when He comes to get His own, He'll have no trouble recognising me . . . my colours will be clear.

Prayer together

Have a time of thanksgiving for who Jesus is and what he has done. You might like to sing some hymns or modern worship songs that are well known to members of your group.

Place a tray with a bread roll and a jug of water and glasses in the centre of the table. Remind the group how Jesus said 'I am the bread of life. Whoever comes to me will never be hungry, and whoever believes in me will never be thirsty . . . anyone who comes to me I will never drive away' (John 6.35,37) and 'those who drink of the water that I will give them will never be thirsty. The water that I will give will become in them a spring of water gushing up to eternal life' (John 4.14). Invite members of the group to come forward in silence to the tray and take a piece of bread and a drink of water as a way of symbolically receiving all that Jesus offers.

Jesus has given himself for us. He invites us to give ourselves afresh to him. You might like to finish by praying together this prayer from the Spiritual Exercises of Ignatius Loyola:

> Take, Lord and receive all my liberty,
> my memory, my understanding, and my entire will –
> all that I have and call my own.
> You have given it all to me.
> To you, Lord, I return it.
> Everything is yours; do with it what you will.
> Give me only your love and your grace.
> This is enough for me.

Putting it into practice

Remind people that, just because this is the last of the meetings for this module, they should not forget to read the last and most exciting part of the Gospel. The passages for this week are Luke 19.45 – 24.53 or John 18.1 – 21.25.

Summary and example timings

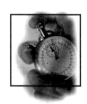

	mins
Group activity: A postcard to a friend	10
Input and discussion: Why Jesus is important	20
Group activity: A resolution to learn more	10
Bible study and discussion: How should we respond to Jesus?	20
Buzz groups: A challenge to discipleship	15
Prayer together	10
Putting it into practice	5

Why Jesus is important

Jesus:

- *shows us what God is like and enables us to know the Father: John 1.18; John 14.6-10, 20-21; Colossians 1.15-20; Hebrews 1.3.*

- *makes it possible for us to be forgiven and start again: Acts 2.38; Romans 6.3-11; 2 Corinthians 5.17-21; 1 John 1.6 – 2.2.*

- *has conquered death and promises we shall be raised: John 11.25-26; 1 Corinthians 15.20-26; 1 Thessalonians 4.13-14.*

- *has promised us the gift of the Holy Spirit: John 7.37-39; Acts 1.4-8; 2.33, 38-39; Romans 8.14-16, 26-27.*

- *promises to be with us at all times and in all circumstances: Matthew 28.18-20; John 14.18-23; Romans 8.35-39.*

- *shows us how to be truly human: John 10.10.*

- *incorporates us into a new family, the Church: Luke 8.19-21; Galatians 4.4-7; Ephesians 3.14-19; 1 Peter 2.9-10.*

- *has broken down the walls that divide people: Galatians 3.27-29; Ephesians 2.8-22.*

- *has taught us how to pray and prays for us: Matthew 6.5-15; Luke 11.1-13; Hebrews 7.25.*

- *feeds and sustains us in our Christian journey: Matthew 11.28-30; John 6.35-40; John 15.4-11.*

- *is Lord of heaven and earth: Philippians 2.5-11; Matthew 28.19-20.*

How should we respond to Jesus?

In the sixth month the angel Gabriel was sent by God to a town in Galilee called Nazareth, to a virgin engaged to a man whose name was Joseph, of the house of David. The virgin's name was Mary. And he came to her and said, 'Greetings, favoured one! The Lord is with you.' But she was much perplexed by his words and pondered what sort of greeting this might be. The angel said to her, 'Do not be afraid, Mary, for you have found favour with God. And now, you will conceive in your womb and bear a son, and you will name him Jesus. He will be great, and will be called the Son of the Most High, and the Lord God will give to him the throne of his ancestor David. He will reign over the house of Jacob for ever, and of his kingdom there will be no end.' Mary said to the angel, 'How can this be, since I am a virgin?' The angel said to her, 'The Holy Spirit will come upon you, and the power of the Most High will overshadow you; therefore the child to be born will be holy; he will be called Son of God. And now, your relative Elizabeth in her old age has also conceived a son; and this is the sixth month for her who was said to be

> barren. For nothing will be impossible with God.' Then Mary said, 'Here am I, the servant of the Lord; let it be with me according to your word.' Then the angel departed from her.
>
> Luke 1.26-38.

Mary was a very ordinary person, a young girl from a humble background. She was confused and frightened by the angel's appearance and greeting. She did not really understand all that God was inviting her to be part of, but she said yes to God.

For many Christians throughout the centuries, Mary has been the model of discipleship, someone who responded to God in loving, trusting obedience. As a result of her 'yes' Christ was born in her. Her role, as the mother of our Lord, was unique. But Paul assures us that Jesus lives in all who put their trust in him (Galatians 2.20; Colossians 1.27). We too are invited to be Christ-bearers. It is as we say yes to God day by day and trust in all that Jesus has done for us, that the life of Jesus is shaped and formed in us as individuals and as his body, the Church. We are able to share him with a needy world.

Prayer together

The following prayer from the Spiritual Exercises of Ignatius Loyola may be used:

> Take, Lord and receive all my liberty,
> my memory, my understanding, and my entire will –
> all that I have and call my own.
> You have given it all to me.
> To you, Lord, I return it.
> Everything is yours; do with it what you will.
> Give me only your love and your grace.
> This is enough for me.

Putting it into practice

Remember to read the last and most exciting part of the Gospel. This week's passages are Luke 19.45 – 24.53 or John 18.1 – 21.25.

Come, Holy Spirit

Introduction

'Come, Holy Spirit' has been the prayer of the Church in every generation. At the beginning of Acts, Luke tells us of Jesus' instructions to his first disciples:

> While staying with them, he ordered them not to leave Jerusalem, but to wait there for the promise of the Father. 'This,' he said, 'is what you have heard from me; for John baptized with water, but you will be baptized with the Holy Spirit not many days from now.'
>
> Acts 1.4-5

From earliest times, especially at Pentecost and at ordination services, the Church has prayed the great hymn, Veni Creator Spiritu, 'Come, Holy Ghost, our souls inspire'. At every confirmation, the bishop prays that each candidate is strengthened and confirmed in faith by the Holy Spirit. In every Eucharist, or Holy Communion, the celebrant cries out to God for the people: 'Renew us by your Spirit'. In the last 30 years this ancient prayer of the Church has been taken up afresh in the songs and choruses originating in charismatic renewal: 'Spirit of the living God, fall afresh on me'.

Christians have always prayed and continue to pray this prayer because, if we are wise, we recognize that we cannot live the Christian life, still less fulfil the mission Christ has given us, without the continual refreshing, renewing and indwelling power of God the Holy Spirit.

This part of *Emmaus* is not meant to be an academic and detached study of the third person of the Trinity. The course is designed to enable the members of your own small group to make the prayer 'Come, Holy Spirit' a very genuine part of their Christian life and experience.

For that reason the key starting-point in this unit is your own prayer, for yourself and each member of the group, that, as you engage with the study material and with one another, the creative, energizing Spirit of God will work in your lives in his gentle, powerful, sovereign way and that you will never be the same again.

You will need to exercise careful discernment that this is the right growth course to offer to your group and in your church at this particular time. As with all the *Emmaus* courses, it is essential that the group and the leaders have the support of the clergy and wider church family. You will also need to reflect carefully in advance on how to handle different parts of the material, particularly the opportunities for prayer.

'Come, Holy Spirit' consists of four main sessions of material, with ideas for how to follow on from the course: a service of renewal, dedication and prayer for one another; and suggestions for members of your group to develop and grow in their use of spiritual gifts as you move on to different subjects for study.

The course as set out here envisages a small group of up to a dozen people engaging with the study over four main sessions of about 90 minutes each. However, it would also be possible, and in many situations helpful, to use the course as the material for a residential weekend or an at-home parish conference over a Friday evening and all day Saturday.

If you choose one of these options, it may be that a larger group of people will be involved: perhaps the course will be offered to the whole parish or to a number of churches together. If there are more than a dozen people taking part, then the teaching input can be done centrally (though, ideally, by more than one person), and the group work should be in huddles of no more than five people with a leader for each. You will need to adapt the material slightly as you go through if it is to be used in this way. A possible structure for a parish conference is given at the end of the leaders' guide.

An overview of the course

Session One: The story of the Holy Spirit gives an account of the Holy Spirit's work in creation and in the Old Testament period; in the life of Jesus and the Apostles and in our lives today. The main biblical source is the teaching on the Spirit in Luke and Acts. The session summarizes and repeats some of the material from Session Five of the *Emmaus* Nurture course.

Session Two: The indwelling Holy Spirit focuses on the teaching of the Spirit in the Gospel of John, on receiving the Holy Spirit and on the great biblical picture of the Holy Spirit as the wind or breath of God.

Session Three: The transforming Holy Spirit draws mainly on Paul's theology of the Spirit. It is about how the Holy Spirit changes us from within and the great picture of the Holy Spirit as water.

Session Four: The empowering Holy Spirit draws on Acts and St Paul. It is an opportunity to look at the empowering and the gifts of the Spirit as we use them today and at the picture of the Holy Spirit as fire.

The section 'Putting it into practice' for each of the four sessions concentrates upon prayer and Bible reading. Different prayers are offered for each group member to use each week. The Bible readings suggested take the group through the book of the Acts of the Apostles (sometimes called the Acts of the Holy Spirit). For this season of time as the group focuses on the work and activity of the Spirit, there may be a need for less activity and more stillness and reflection. It is not a time, therefore, for the group to begin new projects individually or together. In the very early Church, candidates who were baptized at Easter then entered a period from Easter to Pentecost that was about stillness and quiet, learning to appreciate the mysteries they had entered into through baptism. This particular course, in a similar way, is most of all about a deepening of each person's walk with God.

There will be opportunity to pray together and to pray for one another in each session of the course, but the best way to follow on is probably to devote a whole fifth session to worship and prayer together around the prayer 'Come, Holy Spirit'.

Session One: The story of the Holy Spirit

	mins
Bible study and discussion: Acts 19.1-7	10
Buzz groups: Your story of the Holy Spirit	15
Input and discussion: The history of the Holy Spirit	30
Bible study and discussion: The Holy Spirit as a dove	20
Suggestions for prayer together: Come, Holy Ghost, our souls inspire	10
Putting it into practice	5

Session Two: The indwelling Holy Spirit

	mins
Bible study and discussion: John 14.15-27; 16.5-15	10
Buzz groups: The Holy Spirit lives in me	15
Input and discussion: Receiving the Holy Spirit	25
Bible study and exercise: The breath of God	20
Suggestions for prayer together: The breath of Jesus	10
Putting it into practice	5

Session Three: The transforming Holy Spirit

	mins
Bible study and discussion: Galatians 5.16-25	10
Buzz groups: Changing as a Christian	15
Input and discussion: Working with the Holy Spirit	25
Bible study and exercise: The Holy Spirit as water	20
Suggestions for prayer together: Thirsty ground and living water	10
Putting it into practice	5

Session Four: The empowering Holy Spirit

	mins
Bible study and discussion: Luke 24.45-49; Acts 1.1-9	10
Buzz groups: Power for ministry	15
Input and discussion: The power and gifts of the Spirit	40
Bible study and discussion: The Holy Spirit as fire	10
Suggestions for prayer together: Renew us by your Spirit	10
Putting it into practice	5

The story of the Holy Spirit

Bible study and discussion: Acts 19.1-7

Welcome the group and introduce the new material. Emphasize that the course is called 'Come, Holy Spirit' and that the heart of this new unit of *Emmaus* is to welcome the Holy Spirit into individual lives and the life of the group in a deeper and a fuller way.

Depending on where people are coming from in their own understanding of the Holy Spirit, you might want to mention that people are often hesitant or ignorant of the work of the Spirit in the Christian life today. They are not unlike the disciples Paul met in Ephesus when he first arrived in that great city.

Read Acts 19.1-7.

A good way to picture the scene is to imagine Paul asking this tiny group of disciples a number of questions. Perhaps he is going through a simple catechism – a statement of Christian belief in question and answer form. Before the great mission to Ephesus begins, Paul checks that the Christians already there have been fully initiated into the Way.

So the conversation may have gone:

Paul: Do you know about God the Father, who made heaven and earth?

Ephesians: Yes, Paul, we know about him.

Paul: Do you know about the Lord Jesus, about his birth and his life and his ministry?

Ephesians: Yes, Paul. Apollos told us all about him. We are his disciples.

Paul: And do you understand about the death of Jesus on the cross for our sins and his Resurrection from the dead?

Ephesians: Most certainly, Paul. Apollos told us all about baptism for the forgiveness of sins.

Paul: And did you receive the Holy Spirit when you first believed?

Ephesians: No. We haven't even heard that there is a Holy Spirit.

You may like to perform this dialogue as a short sketch.

Many Christians today are not unlike those disciples in Ephesus. We may have spent many years as part of the Church. We may have mentioned the Holy Spirit (or, more likely, the Holy Ghost) in the creed; we may know the story of the day of Pentecost; but we may have heard very little and understood very little and acknowledged very little of the Holy Spirit's work in our lives.

If that is the case, then it needs to be put right.

Paul gave the Ephesian Christians some fuller instruction in the faith. Then he baptized them in the name of Jesus, laid hands on them, and they received the Holy Spirit and spoke in tongues.

In this course we shall be sharing together about our experience of the Holy Spirit. We shall be receiving instruction together. And we shall be praying for one another, sometimes with the laying on of hands, that the Holy Spirit will do a deeper work in our lives. We need to be open that the Spirit will give us new gifts to enable us to build each other up in faith and to grow in love. One of the greatest and best-known passages in Scripture, 1 Corinthians 13, emphasizes that the chief work of the Spirit in our lives is to increase in us the most important gift of love.

There may be some questions or comments the group has arising from the passage or what you have said. Then take a moment to be quiet together and pray for your life together on this part of *Emmaus*.

Buzz groups: Your story of the Holy Spirit

Give people an opportunity to respond to the story about Ephesus by sharing their own experience and knowledge of the Holy Spirit. As you introduce this time, make sure you give people full permission to be able to say: 'I've never even heard that there is a Holy Spirit'; or 'I don't want anything to do with all this tongues and waving hands in the air' or 'I don't know much but I really want to learn more'.

If there are not too many people, try to do the whole thing as one group.

You may want to end with a longer, prepared testimony, given by yourself or by one of the group, or by someone you have invited in for the session. If you can, have someone share a story of a dramatic, life-changing encounter with the Spirit, to encourage the whole group to go deeper with this course.

Input and discussion: The history of the Holy Spirit

The input for this session summarizes the first part of Session Five of the *Emmaus* Nurture course, 'The Holy Spirit'.

If all your group members have recently been through this course, you may want to lessen the time you spend on the input this week and have a longer time of sharing and Bible study. You may be helped in your preparation by reading the leaders' guide for the nurture course for Session Five.

It's worth beginning what you say by mentioning that the Holy Spirit is a person – 'he', not 'it'. He is the third person of the Trinity. As the creed says:

> We believe in the Holy Spirit,
> the Lord, the giver of life,
> who proceeds from the Father and the Son,
> who with the Father and the Son is worshipped and glorified,
> who has spoken through the prophets.

And as we are asked in the service of baptism:

> Do you believe and trust in God the Holy Spirit,
> who gives life to the people of God
> and makes Christ known in the world?

The Holy Spirit is not some optional extra to the main Christian faith. The Spirit is the third person of the Trinity. We need to know about him and to know him.

Trace the story through the following Bible verses (and only go into as much detail as the group is comfortable with). For ease of reference (if a group is unfamiliar with finding lots of passages in different places), the Bible references are printed on a supplementary handout.

- *The Holy Spirit is present and active in creation (Genesis 1.1-2).*

- *In Old Testament days the Holy Spirit was not given to every believer. The Spirit of God rested on great national leaders (like Moses and the elders of Israel – Numbers 11.16-27); great prophets (like Elijah and Elisha – 2 Kings 2.7-18); great kings (like David) and other special individuals.*

- *The coming of the Holy Spirit on these people was a definite event that made a real difference to their lives. The Spirit was given so that they could serve the purpose of God in their generation in mighty ways. Every person's character, gifts and ministry were different, but the same Spirit was given to each.*

- *The prophets foretold a time when God would pour out his Holy Spirit upon all people.*

> Then afterward I will pour out my spirit on all flesh; your sons and your daughters shall prophesy, your old men shall dream dreams, and your young men shall see visions. Even on the male and female slaves, in those days, I will pour out my spirit.
>
> Joel 2.28-29

- *The Holy Spirit was active in the life of John the Baptist, in the same way as with the Old Testament prophets. One of John's key prophecies was that the coming Messiah will 'baptize you with the Holy Spirit' (Luke 3.16). The word 'baptize' means to 'drench'.*

- *The Holy Spirit was active in the conception and Incarnation of Jesus (Luke 1.35).*

- *The Holy Spirit was at work in individuals as they recognized Jesus as the Messiah (Luke 2.25-27).*

- *Jesus gives extensive teaching about the Holy Spirit during his ministry (Luke 11.9-13; John 14, 16). He promises that the Holy Spirit would be poured out on all his disciples after the Resurrection (Luke 24.45-49; Acts 1.4-9).*

- *This is what happened on the day of Pentecost. The disciples' lives were completely transformed (Acts 2.1-13).*

  As with the Old Testament accounts and the baptism of Jesus, the pouring out of the Holy Spirit in Acts was a definite, recognizable experience that made a real difference. You knew when it had happened!

- *All through Acts, the Holy Spirit is given to the disciples either at conversion or in subsequent times of prayer, renewal or commitment (Acts 4.31; 9.17-19; 10.44-46).*

- *The same promise of the Holy Spirit is given to every Christian today.*

> Peter said to them, 'Repent, and be baptized every one of you in the name of Jesus Christ so that your sins may be forgiven; and you will receive the gift of the Holy Spirit. For the promise is for you, for your children, and for all who are far away, everyone whom the Lord our God calls to him.'
>
> Acts 2.38-39

- *The remainder of the New Testament contains many, many references to the powerful work of the Spirit in human lives.*

As you tell the story of the Holy Spirit, give people the chance to interject, to ask questions, to explore some passages a bit more and so on. It may help to summarize the points as you go, on a very simple visual aid. You may want to give the group a chance to huddle in twos and threes at the end of the input to draw out any remaining questions and to check that people have the main outline in their minds.

Bible study and discussion: The Holy Spirit as a dove

Each session of the course explores one of the great biblical pictures of the Spirit's work.

Ask people to divide into smaller groups of no more than four and look together at the story of Jesus' baptism by John in Mark 1.9-11 and John 1.32-34.

The groups should then look at the following questions:

1   Why do you think Mark emphasizes that the heavens were torn open?

2   What do you learn about the Holy Spirit from this picture of a dove?

3   What else do you learn about the Spirit from the passage?

Give the groups about ten minutes together and then draw out the different answers and insights each has received.

One of the things you may want to draw out of the discussion is the gentleness of the Holy Spirit, represented as a dove. Sometimes Christian people can be afraid of the Holy Spirit's work in their lives, thinking that 'empowering' or 'being filled' with the Spirit is like being taken over or swamped by someone outside ourselves. The Holy Spirit is not like that. He is as gentle as a dove.

It is also worth emphasizing that, if Jesus needed a particular gift and anointing as he began his public ministry, how much more do we need that anointing in our lives? The Bible does not suggest that the Holy Spirit was not working within Jesus before his baptism by John. But there still came a time when he needed a particular and definite empowering with the Spirit for his public ministry. We will know such times in our lives as well.

Suggestions for prayer together: Come, Holy Ghost, our souls inspire

Printed on the supplementary handout are two different prayers. You will also find the words in hymn books and songbooks. You may want to use them in the way suggested here, or in some other way:

Light a candle in the centre of the room to indicate that a time of prayer is beginning.

Allow a time of silent prayer, asking each person to reflect on what has been learned this evening and to offer it to God.

Say together the great prayer: 'Come, Holy Ghost, our souls inspire', leaving a gap between each verse for quiet reflection.

You may like to play a recording of the words sung by a choir after you have said them together.

Allow a time of open prayer and petition.

End with the song: 'Spirit of the living God, fall afresh on me'. The song works well unaccompanied if you don't have a musician in the group.

Don't be in too much of a hurry to end the prayer time in this or future sessions. It may be that God will answer your prayer almost immediately and that the Spirit will begin to renew and rekindle love and faith in several members of the group. One of the most important things in welcoming the presence of the Holy Spirit is giving him space and time in which to do his gentle work.

When you sense the right time has come, end the prayers by saying the Grace together.

Putting it into practice

You may want to give a general introduction to the Putting it into practice sections for the course.

The reading set for this week is Acts 1 – 7.

The prayer is an invitation to use one of the songs or hymns each day as a prayer for renewal and the gift of the Spirit.

Invite the group to pray the prayer they choose for one another as well as for themselves.

Summary and example timings

	mins
Bible study and discussion: Acts 19.1-7	10
Buzz groups: Your story of the Holy Spirit	15
Input and discussion: The history of the Holy Spirit	30
Bible study and discussion: The Holy Spirit as a dove	20
Suggestions for prayer together: Come, Holy Ghost, our souls inspire	10
Putting it into practice	5

The story of the Holy Spirit handout

Bible study: Acts 19.1-7

> While Apollos was in Corinth, Paul passed through the interior regions and came to Ephesus, where he found some disciples. He said to them, 'Did you receive the Holy Spirit when you became believers?' They replied, 'No, we have not even heard that there is a Holy Spirit.' Then he said, 'Into what then were you baptized?' They answered, 'Into John's baptism.' Paul said, 'John baptized with the baptism of repentance, telling the people to believe in the one who was to come after him, that is, in Jesus.' On hearing this, they were baptized in the name of the Lord Jesus. When Paul had laid his hands on them, the Holy Spirit came upon them, and they spoke in tongues and prophesied – altogether there were about twelve of them.

The passage describes what happens when Paul first met the disciples in Ephesus.

He probably asked them a series of questions to discover where they were spiritually and what they had learned.

Many Christians today are like the Ephesian disciples. We may have spent many years as part of the Church. We may have mentioned the Holy Spirit (or, more likely, the Holy Ghost) in the creed; we may know the story of the day of Pentecost; but we may have heard very little and understood very little and acknowledged very little of the Holy Spirit's work in our lives.

Your story of the Holy Spirit

Share together your own understanding and experience of the Holy Spirit in the Christian life.

- *Who is he?*

- *Have you experienced his work in your own life?*

- *Have you any experience of the gifts of the Holy Spirit working in your life or in the lives of those you know?*

The history of the Holy Spirit

The Nicene Creed says:

> We believe in the Holy Spirit,
> the Lord, the giver of life,
> who proceeds from the Father and the Son,
> who with the Father and the Son is worshipped and glorified.
> who has spoken through the prophets.

The service of baptism asks:

> Do you believe and trust in God the Holy Spirit, who gives life to the people of God and makes Christ known in the world?

- *The Holy Spirit is present in creation (Genesis 1.1-2).*

- *In Old Testament days, the Holy Spirit was not given to every believer. The Spirit of God rested on great national leaders; great prophets; great kings.*

- *The coming of the Holy Spirit on these people was a definite event that made a real difference to their lives.*

- *The prophets foretold a time when God would pour out his Holy Spirit upon all people (Joel 2.28-29).*

- *The Holy Spirit was active in the life of John the Baptist, in the same way as with the Old Testament prophets.*

- *The Holy Spirit was active in the conception and Incarnation of Jesus.*

- *The Holy Spirit was at work in individuals as they recognized Jesus as the Messiah (Luke 2.25-27).*

- *Jesus gives extensive teaching about the Holy Spirit during his ministry (Luke 11.9-13; John 14, 16). He promises that the Holy Spirit would be poured out on all his disciples after the Resurrection (Luke 24.45-49; Acts 1.4-9).*

- *This is what happened on the day of Pentecost. The disciples' lives were completely transformed (Acts 2.1-13).*
  As with the Old Testament accounts and the baptism of Jesus, the pouring out of the Holy Spirit in Acts was a definite, recognizable experience that made a real difference. You knew when it had happened!

- *All through Acts, the Holy Spirit is given to the disciples either at conversion or in subsequent times of prayer, renewal or commitment (Acts 4.31; 9.17-19; 10.44-46).*

- *The same promise of the Holy Spirit is given to every Christian today (Acts 2.38-39).*

The Holy Spirit as a dove

Look at the story of Jesus' baptism by John in Mark 1.9-11 and John 1.32-34.

1   Why do you think Mark emphasizes that the heavens were torn open?
2   What do you learn about the Holy Spirit from this picture of a dove?
3   What else do you learn about the Spirit from the passage?

Putting it into practice

The reading set for this week is Acts 1 – 7.

Use one of the songs or hymns each day as a prayer for renewal and the gift of the Spirit.

Pray the prayer you choose for one another as well as for yourself.

The story of the Holy Spirit

A selection of Bible passages

Genesis 1.1-2

In the beginning when God created the heavens and the earth, the earth was a formless void and darkness covered the face of the deep, while a wind from God swept over the face of the waters.

Joel 2.28-29

Then afterward I will pour out my spirit on all flesh; your sons and your daughters shall prophesy, your old men shall dream dreams, and your young men shall see visions. Even on the male and female slaves, in those days, I will pour out my spirit.

Luke 2.25-28

Now there was a man in Jerusalem whose name was Simeon; this man was righteous and devout, looking forward to the consolation of Israel, and the Holy Spirit rested on him. It had been revealed to him by the Holy Spirit that he would not see death before he had seen the Lord's Messiah. Guided by the Spirit, Simeon came into the temple; and when the parents brought in the child Jesus, to do for him what was customary under the law, Simeon took him in his arms and praised God.

Luke 11.9-13

So, I say to you, Ask, and it will be given you; search, and you will find; knock, and the door will be opened for you. For everyone who asks receives, and everyone who searches finds, and for everyone who knocks, the door will be opened. Is there anyone among you who, if your child asks for a fish, will give a snake instead of a fish? Or if the child asks for an egg, will give a scorpion? If you then, who are evil, know how to give good gifts to your children, how much more will the heavenly Father give the Holy Spirit to those who ask him!

John 14. 16

And I will ask the Father, and he will give you another Advocate, to be with you forever.

Luke 24.45-49

Then he opened their minds to understand the scriptures, and he said to them, 'Thus it is written, that the Messiah is to suffer and to rise from the dead on the third day, and that repentance and forgiveness of sins is to be proclaimed in his name to all nations, beginning from Jerusalem. You are witnesses of these things. And see, I am sending upon you what my Father promised; so stay here in the city until you have been clothed with power from on high.'

Acts 1.4-9

While staying with them, he ordered them not to leave Jerusalem, but to wait there for the promise of the Father. 'This' he said, 'is what you have heard from me; for John baptized with water, but you will be baptized with the Holy Spirit not many days from now.' So when they had come together, they asked him, 'Lord, is this the time when you will restore the kingdom to Israel?' He replied, 'It is not for you to know the times or periods that the Father has set by his own authority. But you will receive power when the Holy Spirit has come upon you; and you will be my witnesses in Jerusalem, in all Judea and Samaria, and to the ends of the earth.' When he had said this, as they were watching, he was lifted up, and a cloud took him out of their sight.

Acts 2.1-4

When the day of Pentecost had come, they were all together in one place. And suddenly from heaven there came a sound like the rush of a violent wind, and it filled the entire house where they were sitting. Divided tongues, as of fire, appeared among them, and a tongue rested on each of them. All of them were filled with the Holy Spirit and began to speak in other languages, as the Spirit gave them ability.

Acts 4.31

When they had prayed, the place in which they were gathered together was shaken; and they were all filled with the Holy Spirit and spoke the word of God with boldness.

Acts 9.17-19

So Ananias went and entered the house. He laid his hands on Saul and said, 'Brother Saul, the Lord Jesus, who appeared to you on your way here, has sent me so that you may regain your sight and be filled with the Holy Spirit.' And immediately something like scales fell from his eyes, and his sight was restored. Then he got up and was baptized, and after taking some food, he regained his strength.

Acts 10.44-46

While Peter was still speaking, the Holy Spirit fell upon all who heard the word. The circumcised believers who had come with Peter were astounded that the gift of the Holy Spirit had been poured out even on the Gentiles, for they heard them speaking in tongues and extolling God. Then Peter said, 'Can anyone withhold the water for baptizing these people who have received the Holy Spirit just as we have?' So he ordered them to be baptized in the name of Jesus Christ. Then they invited him to stay for several days.

Acts 2.38-39

Peter said to them, 'Repent, and be baptized every one of you in the name of Jesus Christ so that your sins may be forgiven; and you will receive the gift of the Holy Spirit. For the promise is for you, for your children, and for all who are far away, everyone whom the Lord our God calls to him.'

Mark 1.9-11

In those days Jesus came from Nazareth of Galilee and was baptized by John in the Jordan. And just as he was coming up out of the water, he saw the heavens torn apart and the Spirit descending like a dove on him. And a voice came from heaven, 'You are my Son, the Beloved; with you I am well pleased.'

John 1.32-34

And John testified, 'I saw the Spirit descending from heaven like a dove, and it remained on him. I myself did not know him, but the one who sent me to baptize with water said to me, "He on whom you see the Spirit descend and remain is the one who baptizes with the Holy Spirit." And I myself have seen and have testified that this is the Son of God.'

The story of
the Holy Spirit

Suggestions for prayer

Come, Holy Ghost, our souls inspire

Come, Holy Ghost, our souls inspire,
And lighten with celestial fire;
Thou the anointing Spirit art,
Who dost thy sevenfold gifts impart.

Thy blessed unction from above
Is comfort, life and fire of love;
Enable with perpetual light
The dullness of our blinded sight.

Anoint and cheer our soiled face
With the abundance of thy grace:
Keep far our foes, give peace at home;
Where thou art guide no ill can come.

Teach us to know the Father, Son,
And thee, of Both, to be but One;
That through the ages all along,
This may be our endless song:

Praise to thy eternal merit,
Father, Son and Holy Spirit. Amen.

J. Cosin, after R. Maurus

Spirit of the Living God,
fall afresh on me;
Spirit of the Living God
fall afresh on me.
Break me, melt me,
mould me, fill me
Spirit of the Living God,
fall afresh on me.

The indwelling Holy Spirit

Bible study: John 14.15-27; John 16.5-15

Welcome the group and open in prayer. You may want to begin with asking for any reflections, questions or stories that have arisen from Session One or the ongoing prayer and Bible reading. Again, be open to the truth that God may be answering the group's prayers in ways you do not expect.

Recap briefly on last week and introduce the theme for this session: when we become Christians, God's promise is that the Holy Spirit comes to live in us and dwell within us. Today we explore what that means.

Explain the context of the Bible passages the group will be looking at to begin the evening: John sets a great deal of Jesus' teaching about the Christian life in a series of discourses at the Last Supper. We are going to look briefly together at two passages from these last discourses.

Divide the group in half and ask each small group to take one of the passages; read it together and draw out what that particular passage teaches about the work and person of the Holy Spirit.

Allow up to ten minutes for the small group Bible study and then another five minutes for each group to share its findings with the other.

Note that different English translations of the Bible differ on the words they use to translate these passages, particularly for the Greek word 'paraclete'. The word literally means 'one who draws alongside'. NIV has 'counsellor'; GNB uses 'helper'; NEB and NRSV have 'advocate'. You could also use 'encourager' or even 'coach'. This is one Bible study where it will be helpful to compare translations and where you might like to look up a simple commentary before the meeting.

Try to summarize the Bible study by writing down as a series of bullet points on a flip chart (or a large piece of paper on the floor) what the groups discover about the Spirit. People can then copy these down on to the space in their handouts. Some of the bullets you should have are:

John 14.15-27

■ *He is the Advocate (what does that mean?).*

■ *He will be with you for ever.*

■ *He lives with you and will be in you.*

■ *He is sent by the Father in Jesus' name.*

■ *He will teach you all things.*

■ *He will remind you of all I have said to you.*

John 16.5-15

■ *He will convict the world in regard to sin.*

■ *In regard to righteousness.*

■ *In regard to judgement.*

Some explanation may be needed here. The Spirit coming into the life of a Christian affects the world – those around us who are not yet Christians.

Occasionally a person who becomes a Christian can become the victim of quite bitter persecution within his or her own family or workplace or community. Sometimes that persecution can be caused, at least partly, by the Christian's own misplaced zeal to go on and on about his or her new faith. But more often it is that the Holy Spirit, who now dwells in the Christian, is beginning to 'convict' the non-Christians around about sin, about righteousness and about judgement. For that reason the non-Christians feel uncomfortable around the new Christian and can make life unpleasant: a reaction to the Holy Spirit's presence in their lives.

- ■   *He will guide you into all truth.*

Buzz groups: The Holy Spirit lives in me

Talk with one another, in one large group if possible, of any ways in which you have identified the Holy Spirit's presence in your life:

- ■   *Are there any times when you have felt convicted of sin, righteousness or judgement, either before or after you became a Christian? Has your conscience become softer? Do things that used to seem OK seem now to be wrong?*

- ■   *Do you have a sense of the Holy Spirit not only working in you from time to time but dwelling within you? How are you aware of his presence?*

- ■   *Have you known times when the Holy Spirit is guiding you; reminding you of words from Scripture; giving you the right words to use in a difficult situation and so on?*

Again you may want to follow this time of informal sharing with a time of prepared personal testimony, asking one of the group or a visitor to share in more depth.

Bear in mind during this time of sharing that some people may want to remain silent, either because they don't want to expose their own lack of experience in these areas or because some things are too deep for words. Give people permission not to join in the time of sharing.

During the discussion try to avoid, if you can, any sense that a particular experience or set of experiences is 'normative' in the Christian life – and you're not a 'proper' Christian unless this or that has happened to you. God moves in different people in different ways through his endlessly creative Spirit.

Input and discussion: Receiving the Holy Spirit

As with Session One, the main input is based on the teaching given in Session Five of the *Emmaus* Nurture course. If your group has taken part in that course recently, you may be able to move through the teaching given here more quickly.

I Is the Holy Spirit at work in every Christian?

Yes, he is. Paul writes that no one can say 'Jesus is Lord' except by the Holy Spirit (1 Corinthians 12.3). Even before you became a Christian, God was at work in your life in many ways – and he has continued to work by his Spirit since then.

Is this something with which you can identify?

Leaders should note that, in classical Pentecostal teaching, and some streams of charismatic renewal, a very rigid, two-stage picture of Christian initiation has been developed:

1   A person receives Christ as Saviour.

2   At a subsequent stage and time, he or she receives the baptism of the Holy Spirit, which is made evident by the gift of tongues.

Where new or established Christians have been exposed to this kind of teaching it can have a negative effect of producing a feeling that there are first- and second-class Christians. One of the other side-effects can be that people who have received something like a second experience of the Spirit's work can actually be quite closed to the continual work of the Spirit in their lives from year to year.

Although this pattern does fit some people's experience, it does not by any means fit everyone, nor is it easy to reconcile with the New Testament, which describes many different journeys and spiritual experiences.

If this Pentecostal teaching is not a problem for your group, don't feel you have to raise it. If it is, you should take time to explore it and lead people on from it.

2   Is there a definite experience of baptism (or drenching) in the Holy Spirit?

Yes, there is. The Bible speaks of this experience and it is part of the Christian life today. Jesus experienced such an anointing by the Holy Spirit at his baptism (Luke 3.22) even though the Holy Spirit was active in his life before. The disciples experienced the work and power of the Spirit before Pentecost, but they still needed the empowering at Pentecost before their new ministry could begin.

Some Christians go to the opposite extreme from the Pentecostals and deny the reality of any dramatic or gradual experience of the Spirit's life and power at or subsequent to becoming a Christian.

Again, this view does not match the New Testament witness or the clear experience of many Christian people today who continually encounter the life-changing power of God the Holy Spirit in a whole range of different ways.

Are there people in the group who can identify with this kind of deep and dramatic experience of the Spirit's power?

3   When should I expect this kind of renewing work of the Spirit to happen?

At the time that is right for you. We can't put the Holy Spirit in a box. He's in charge. For some people there is a definite experience of the Holy Spirit at conversion, or near to that point. For other people there is a definite experience of the Holy Spirit's empowering months, or years, later. For others, both conversion and being filled with the Spirit happen gradually and slowly over a long period of time.

The experience you have of God's presence in your life now is more important than the way you received it.

At this stage it may be worth looking briefly at John 3.8. How can we contain or dictate to the wind, the breath of God?

4   Is this a once and for all event?

No. There's much more to come. Paul tells the Ephesian Christians to go on being filled with the Spirit (Ephesians 5.18). The disciples are filled with the Spirit over and over again in Acts. The process of being renewed by the Holy Spirit goes on until we are with the Lord.

5 Can we reject God's blessing for us?

We can and many do.

The Bible speaks of Christians who grieve the Spirit (Ephesians 4.30); insult the Spirit (Hebrews 10.29) and put out the Spirit's fire (1 Thessalonians 5.19).

Our relationship with the Holy Spirit is a relationship. We need to play our part: receiving and welcoming the Spirit's work in us.

6 How do we receive the gift of the Holy Spirit?

We simply ask (Luke 11.9-13). The asking happens through prayer, by ourselves or with others. Often in the rhythm of our Christian lives we will experience times of spiritual dryness followed by seasons of refreshing and renewal. We are often helped in being refreshed and renewed in the sense of God's presence in our lives by the prayers of other Christians and through the ministry of laying on of hands.

It may be especially appropriate for Christians to seek God for a deeper experience of the Spirit's presence at the following times:

■ *Near the beginning of their Christian life.*

■ *At or around a service of baptism, confirmation or renewal of vows.*

■ *Before taking on some major new ministry or taking a new step in their life.*

■ *After a time of extended spiritual dryness.*

7 How do I know I have received the Holy Spirit?

If we are people in whom the Spirit has been moving gradually in our lives over the years, we may not always know whether we have received the Holy Spirit. We do not necessarily feel any different.

Paul tells us that the work of the Holy Spirit can be told by the fruit that is produced. This is the best test. If your life in Christ is bearing fruit, then you have received the Holy Spirit.

Bible study and exercise: The breath of God

One of the great pictures of the Spirit in the Bible is the picture of the Spirit as the wind or breath of God.

In Hebrew, the words for 'spirit', 'breath' and 'wind' are all the same.

Read together the following passages:

Ezekiel 37.1-14

John 3.8

John 20.19-22

Acts 2.1-4

What do you learn as a group from this picture of the Spirit as the wind or breath of God?

In discussion draw out the following points:

■ *The Spirit is as essential to our Christian lives as breathing is to the life of our bodies: the Holy Spirit gives us spiritual life.*

■ *We can no more contain or fully understand the work of the Holy Spirit than we can follow the wind.*

■ *There is a great range to the Spirit's work: from a gentle breath on the forehead to a mighty wind that shakes the building. The Spirit may work in different people in different ways (and in the same people in different ways at different times).*

If you have time, take a moment to look at the two hymns on the handout, both based on the Holy Spirit as the breath or wind of God.

■ *What allusions can you see in the hymns?*

■ *Which prayer do you prefer?*

Suggestions for prayer together: The breath of Jesus

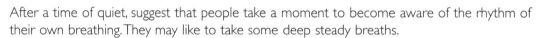

Again, light a candle in the centre of the room.

Ask people to spend a few moments being quiet and still and inviting the presence of the Holy Spirit through silent prayer.

After a time of quiet, suggest that people take a moment to become aware of the rhythm of their own breathing. They may like to take some deep steady breaths.

Ask the group to remember the presence of Jesus in the room.

Read aloud John 20.19-21.

Picture Jesus going from person to person, breathing softly on the forehead of each member of the group and saying to them: 'N, receive the Holy Spirit'. You may want to say these words aloud to each person in the group.

Continue in quiet prayer, asking the group to pray the prayer 'Come, Holy Spirit' in the rhythm of their breathing.

From this point, pray for as long as seems right, as you believe God is leading you – but be aware of any members of the group who may be uncomfortable or not taking part in the prayer.

End with one of the two hymns printed on the supplementary handout. Either say the hymn together or sing the words unaccompanied.

Putting it into practice

It may be appropriate to offer to meet to talk with any members of the group who still have questions after this week's session. Or offer to meet for prayer. Be sensitive to what God is doing.

Suggest that people try to read the next section of Acts in the coming week and that they continue to pray the great words of the hymn.

Summary and example timings

	mins
Bible study and discussion: John 14.15-27; 16.5-15	20
Buzz groups: The Holy Spirit lives in me	10
Input and discussion: Receiving the Holy Spirit	25
Bible study and exercise: The breath of God	20
Suggestions for prayer together: The breath of Jesus	15
Putting it into practice	5

The indwelling Holy Spirit

John 14.15-27

John 16.5-15

The Holy Spirit lives in me

How have you identified the Holy Spirit's presence in your life?

- *Have you ever felt convicted of sin, righteousness or judgement, before or after you became a Christian? Has your conscience become softer? Do things that used to seem OK now seem wrong?*

- *Do you have a sense of the Holy Spirit working in you and dwelling within you? How are you aware of his presence?*

- *Have you known the Holy Spirit guiding you; reminding you of words from Scripture; giving you the right words to use in a difficult situation and so on?*

Receiving the Holy Spirit

1   Is the Holy Spirit at work in every Christian?

Yes. Paul writes that no one can say 'Jesus is Lord' except by the Holy Spirit (1 Corinthians 12.3).

God was at work in your life before you became a Christian and has continued to work by his Spirit since then.

2   Is there a definite experience of baptism (or drenching) in the Holy Spirit?

Yes. The Bible speaks of this and it is part of the Christian life today. Jesus experienced such an anointing at his baptism. The disciples were empowered by the Spirit at Pentecost. The Holy Spirit had already been at work in the lives of Jesus and his disciples before this.

3   When should I expect this kind of renewing work of the Spirit to happen?

When it is right for you. The Holy Spirit is in charge.

The experience you have of God's presence in your life now is more important than the way you received it.

4   Is this a once and for all event?

No. There's much more to come. Paul tells the Ephesian Christians to go on being filled with the Spirit.

5   Can we reject God's blessing for us?

We can and many do. It is possible to grieve him (Ephesians 4.30); outrage him (Hebrews 10.29); and put out the Spirit's fire (1 Thessalonians 5.19).

We need to receive and welcome the Holy Spirit's work in us.

6   How do we receive the gift of the Holy Spirit?

We simply ask.

> So, I say to you, Ask, and it will be given you; search, and you will find; knock, and the door will be opened for you. For everyone who asks receives, and everyone who searches finds, and for everyone who knocks, the door will be opened. Is there anyone among you who, if your child asks for a fish, will give a snake instead of a fish? Or if the child asks for an egg, will give a scorpion? If you then, who are evil, know how to give good gifts to your children, how much more will the heavenly Father give the Holy Spirit to those who ask him!
>
> *Luke 11.9-13*

The asking happens through prayer, alone or with others. It may be especially appropriate to seek God for a deeper experience of the Spirit's presence at the following times:

- *Near the beginning of your Christian life.*

- *At or around a service of baptism, confirmation or renewal of vows.*

- *Before taking on some new ministry or taking a new step in your life.*

- *After a time of extended spiritual dryness.*

7   How do I know I have received the Holy Spirit?

If the Spirit has been moving gradually in our lives over the years, we may not always know whether we have received the Holy Spirit. We may not feel any different.

Paul tells us that the work of the Holy Spirit can be told by the fruit produced. This is the best test. If your life in Christ is bearing fruit then you have received the Holy Spirit.

The breath of God

One of the great pictures of the Spirit in the Bible is as the wind or breath of God.

In Hebrew the words for 'spirit', 'breath' and 'wind' are all the same.

Read:

- *Ezekiel 37.1-14*

- *John 20.19-22*

- *Acts 2.1-4.*

What do you learn from this about the Spirit as the wind or breath of God?

The breath of Jesus

John 20.19-21

> When it was evening on that day, the first day of the week, and the doors of the house where the disciples had met were locked for fear of the Jews, Jesus came and stood among them and said, 'Peace be with you.' After he said this, he showed them his hands and his side. Then the disciples rejoiced when they saw the Lord. Jesus said to them again, 'Peace be with you. As the Father has sent me, so I send you.'

Putting it into practice

The Bible reading for this week is Acts 8 – 14.

Use one of the songs or hymns each day as a prayer for renewal and the gift of the Spirit.

Pray the prayer you choose for one another as well as for yourself.

The indwelling Holy Spirit

Suggestions for prayer together

Breathe on me, Breath of God,
fill me with life anew,
that I may love what thou dost love,
and do what thou wouldst do.

Breathe on me, Breath of God,
until my heart is pure;
until with thee I will one will,
to do and to endure.

Breathe on me, Breath of God,
till I am wholly thine;
until this earthly part of me
glows with thy fire divine.

Breathe on me, Breath of God:
so shall I never die,
but live with thee the perfect life
of thine eternity.

Edwin Hatch

O Breath of life, come sweeping through us,
revive your church with life and power;
O Breath of life, come, cleanse, renew us
and fit your church to meet this hour.

O Breath of love, come breathe within us,
renewing thought and will and heart;
come, love of Christ, afresh to win us,
revive your church in every part!

O Wind of God, come bend us, break us
till humbly we confess our need;
then, in your tenderness remake us,
revive, restore – for this we plead.

Revive us Lord, is zeal abating,
while harvest fields are vast and white?
Revive us Lord, the world is waiting;
equip thy church to spread the light.

Elizabeth A. P. Head, Copyright © controlled

Emmaus Growth course supplementary handout: The indwelling Holy Spirit

The transforming Holy Spirit

Bible study and discussion: Galatians 5.16-25

Again review the Putting it into practice from the last session. You might want to begin by asking the group to share if there are any ways in which members have been more aware of the Holy Spirit dwelling within them since you were last together.

The Holy Spirit comes to dwell within us not only to guide us and to teach us but also to change us and transform us from within.

This is one of the main differences between Christianity and many other faiths and ways of living, which often teach very high ideals and have a great many rules and regulations but which offer their followers little or no help in changing from the inside.

Jesus promises to those who follow him that his Spirit will dwell within us, transforming and changing us to be like Christ. So our faith will be and become not a matter of keeping outward rules and regulations but of being transformed, renewed and changed from the inside.

Read together Galatians 5.16-25.

Ask the group to examine the passage in small groups of three or four and try to work out what it means and especially what it teaches about the Spirit's work. Then ask each group to share what it has discovered with the others.

During the discussion you may want to draw out the following points:

■   *Paul is writing to Christians who have tried to turn Christianity back into a religion of keeping rules and laws.*

■   *He argues that keeping rules is never enough. It is what is inside us that needs to change: our old, sinful nature.*

■   *When we become Christians, the Spirit comes to dwell within us. But we find that the Spirit and our old sinful nature are often in conflict with each other. There is a battle within.*

■   *If we consistently follow the desires of our sinful nature, then certain consequences and actions will follow from that (vv.19-21). These actions will demonstrate that we have not fully surrendered to Christ.*

■   *But if we follow the way of the Spirit, then the fruit of the Holy Spirit will be formed in us: love, joy, peace, patience, kindness, goodness, faithfulness, gentleness, self-control – the character of Christ.*

Buzz groups: Changing as a Christian

It would be good to have a prepared testimony again this week – only this time to begin the sharing time. Ask one of the group or a guest to look back over the time he or she has been a Christian and share, if possible, ways in which change and transformation have happened from within.

Then ask all the group members to share their experience of this kind of inner transformation, around the list on the handout.

Input and discussion: Working with the Holy Spirit

All members of the group will be familiar with the idea that becoming a Christian is a journey or a process. It happens over time.

In the same way, growing more like Jesus is also a process: something that takes the whole of our lives. We call this part of being a Christian 'sanctification'.

In thinking through just how we grow more like Christ, we need to take care to avoid two extremes.

As you go through this next section with the group, make a simple visual aid. At the top of a large piece of paper, write 'sanctification'. On the left-hand side, write the words, 'It happens automatically'.

■   *Some Christians have taught that the whole business of sanctification is automatic. It just happens because the Holy Spirit is living in us. That means we don't need to pay any attention to our behaviour. We can do just as we please. We don't need any rules or guidelines for our conduct because we have been set free in Christ.*

This was part of the teaching in the Church in Corinth. Read 1 Corinthians 6.9-20. The Corinthian Christians were saying: 'Everything is permissible for me' – so all kinds of conduct were permitted in the Church.

Ask the group: 'What do you think is wrong with this approach?' and see what response you get.

The Holy Spirit comes to work within us to change us: but he does not come to dwell in us in order to override our free will or our character. We still need both the Scriptures and the tradition and the teaching of the Church to guide us in the conduct of our lives.

On the right-hand side of the paper write the words: 'It happens through keeping rules'.

■   *Other Christians have taught that being holy comes about through keeping lots and lots of rules and regulations: in other words, through outward observation, not inward change.*

As we saw earlier, this is what was being taught to the Church in Galatia. The new converts were being expected to keep the whole of the Jewish law and to be circumcised as a sign that they were willing to do so.

Read the passage just before the one you read at the beginning: Galatians 5.1-15.

Ask the group: 'What do you think is wrong with this approach?' (expecting holiness to come through keeping rules). See what response you get.

Keeping rules does not bring about the kind of holiness Christians are seeking, which is an inward transformation. At its worst, the keeping of lots and lots of tiny rules produces people like the Pharisees of the Bible.

In the centre of the piece of paper write the words, 'Working together with the Holy Spirit'.

■   *The true Christian teaching on how we grow in the faith is that we are called to work in partnership with the Holy Spirit as he changes our lives from within. Growing in holiness is part of our relationship with God and happens as he works in us.*

That means it is a different process for every single person. And the whole of our life is involved, not simply our outward actions.

One picture from the Pacific Islands puts it this way. A man keeps two dogs in a cave. These two dogs are in continual conflict with one another and are compared to the Holy Spirit dwelling in us, in conflict with our old, sinful nature (Galatians 5.17). The man has a choice about which dog he feeds. The dog that is fed and nourished will grow stronger and will gain the upper hand over the animal that is starved.

In the same way we have a choice. If we feed and indulge the sinful nature within us, that will grow stronger and gain the upper hand. The fruits will become obvious to everyone. But if we nourish and sustain the life of the Holy Spirit within us, through prayer and worship, through Scripture, the Eucharist and Christian fellowship, then the life of the Spirit within us will grow and deepen and the fruit of the Spirit will form in our lives.

If you have time, end this part of the session by asking the group to think about two questions:

1   What are the most important things we can do to nurture and strengthen the Holy Spirit's work within us?

2   The Apostles in Acts 15 provide a very simple list of four guidelines for new Gentile Christians (Acts 15.24-29). If you had to draw up a similar list for a new Christian today, what would you include?

Bible study and exercise: The Holy Spirit as water

Begin by asking what passages or images group members can think of where the Holy Spirit is compared to water.

As part of your own preparation, get hold of a Bible concordance and look up words such as 'water', 'thirst' and 'rain'.

Remind the group of the climate in Israel: nothing grows at all there without water. Rain falls only at certain times of year. That means artificial irrigation is vital for crops and flowers to grow.

Don't introduce too much new material, but you may want to refer briefly to the following passages, especially the last:

■   *Psalms that express a longing for God in terms of thirst for water (especially Psalms 42; 63).*

■   *Ezekiel's picture of the stream flowing from the Temple (Ezekiel 47.1-12).*

■   *Jesus' words about living water (John 4.10-14).*

■   *Jesus' promise of a spring within each Christian (John 7.37-39).*

Think together about why the Holy Spirit is compared to water, and what we learn from this image.

If you have time, end the section with the story of the keeper of the spring, on the supplementary handout.

Ask someone in the group to read the story aloud, and then reflect together on the two questions below.

The story has two levels of meaning:

1   What does it say about the influence of Christians in society as a whole (as salt and light)?

2   What does it say to you about the flow of the river of life within your own life at the present time? Who is the keeper of the spring within your heart?

Suggestions for prayer together: Thirsty ground and living water

Spend some moments in quietness and stillness together, reflecting on your own dryness and thirst for God, using the words from the psalms either said together or individually.

You may want to read aloud the promises from Scripture printed on the supplementary handout.

Then welcome the presence of the Holy Spirit.

Ask the Spirit to unblock the stream of living water within each person, wherever and however it has become restricted.

Again, this could be through silence or open prayer.

Putting it into practice

Again, suggest that the group goes on using the Scriptures and prayer from the handout each day this week and continues to read Acts 15 – 21.

This may also be a good time to prepare the group for the way you intend handling Session Four of the course.

Summary and example timings

	mins
Bible study and discussion: Galatians 5.16-25	10
Buzz groups: Changing as a Christian	15
Input and discussion: Working with the Holy Spirit	30
Bible study and exercise: The Holy Spirit as water	20
Suggestions for prayer together: Thirsty ground and living water	10
Putting it into practice	5

The transforming Holy Spirit

Bible study: Galatians 5.16-25

The Holy Spirit comes to dwell within us not only to guide us and to teach us but also to change us and transform us from within.

This is one of the main differences between Christianity and many other faiths and ways of living, which often teach very high ideals and have a great many rules and regulations but offer to their followers little or no help in changing from the inside.

Jesus promises to those who follow him that his Spirit will dwell within us, transforming and changing us to be like Christ.

Read Galatians 5.16-25.

What do you think the passage means and what does it teach about the Spirit's work?

Changing as a Christian

Since you became a Christian, have your life and character been different?

Have you found any changes in:

- *your temper?*

- *the language you use?*

- *habits of eating and drinking?*

- *the way you spend your time?*

- *the way you shop and spend your money?*

- *your relationships with other people?*

- *attitudes to those who mistreat you?*

- *behaviour at work (honesty, timekeeping and so on)?*

- *things you do now you never did before?*

- *things you have stopped doing that you used to do?*

- *what you watch on television or what you read?*

- *your giving to charity or service in the community?*

Working with the Holy Spirit

Growing more like Jesus is also a process: something that takes the whole of our lives. We call this part of being a Christian 'sanctification'.

In thinking through just how we grow more like Christ, we need to take care to avoid two extremes.

- *Some Christians have taught that the whole business of sanctification is automatic. It just happens because the Holy Spirit is living in us. That means we don't need to pay any attention to our behaviour. We can do just as we please. We don't need any rules or guidelines for our conduct because we have been set free in Christ.*

What do you think is wrong with this approach?

- *Other Christians have taught that being holy comes about through keeping lots and lots of rules and regulations: in other words through outward observation, not inward change.*

What do you think is wrong with this approach?

The true Christian teaching on how we grow in holiness is that we are called to work in partnership with the Holy Spirit as he changes our lives from within. Growing in holiness is part of our relationship with God and happens as he works in us.

That means it is a different process for every single person. And the whole of our life is involved, not simply our outward actions.

1   What are the most important things we can do to nurture and strengthen the Holy Spirit's work within us?

2   The Apostles in Acts 15 provide a very simple list of four guidelines for new Gentile Christians (Acts 15.24-29).

If you had to draw up a similar list for new Christians today, what would you include?

The Holy Spirit as water

Think together about why the Holy Spirit is compared to water, and what we learn from this image. You may like to explore some of the following passages now or in the week to come.

- *Psalms that express a longing for God in terms of thirst for water (especially Psalms 42; 63).*

- *Ezekiel's picture of the stream flowing from the temple (Ezekiel 47.1-12).*

- *Jesus' words about living water (John 4.10-14).*

- *Jesus' promise of a spring within each Christian (John 7.37-39).*

Suggestions for prayer: Thirsty ground and living water

Spend some moments in quietness and stillness together, reflecting on your own dryness and thirst for God, using the words from the Psalms either said together or individually.

Read aloud the promises from Scripture.

Then welcome the presence of the Holy Spirit.

Ask him to unblock the stream of living water within each person, wherever and however it has become restricted.

Putting it into practice

Go on using the Scriptures and prayer from the handout each day this week and go on reading Acts 15 – 21.

The transforming Holy Spirit

The keeper of the spring

A quiet forest dweller lived high above an Austrian village along the eastern slopes of the Alps. The old gentleman had been hired many years ago by a young town council to clear away the debris from the pools of water up in the mountain crevices that fed the lovely spring flowing through their town. With faithful, silent regularity he patrolled the hills, removed the leaves and branches and wiped away the silt that would otherwise choke and contaminate the fresh flow of water. By and by, the village became a popular attraction for vacationers. Graceful swans floated along the crystal clear spring, the millwheels of various businesses located near the water turned day and night, farmlands were naturally irrigated, and the view from the restaurants was picturesque beyond description.

Years passed. One evening the town council met for its semi-annual meeting. As they reviewed the budget, one man's eye caught the salary figure being paid to the obscure keeper of the spring. Said the keeper of the purse: 'Who is the old man? Why do we keep him on year after year? No one ever sees him. For all we know the strange ranger of the hills is doing us no good. He isn't necessary any longer!' By a unanimous vote, they dispensed with the old man's services.

For several weeks, nothing changed. By early autumn, the trees began to shed their leaves. Small branches snapped off and fell into the pools, hindering the rushing flow of sparkling water. One afternoon, someone noticed a slight yellowish brown tint in the spring. A couple of days later the water was much darker. Within another week, a slimy film covered sections of the water along the banks and a foul odour was soon detected. The millwheels moved slower, some finally ground to a halt. Swans left, as did the tourists. Clammy fingers of disease and sickness reached deeply into the village.

Quickly, the embarrassed council called a special meeting. Realising their gross error of judgement, they hired back the old keeper of the spring . . . and within a few weeks the veritable river of life began to clear up. The wheels started to turn and new life returned to the hamlet in the Alps once again.

Charles R. Swindoll, *Improving your serve*, Hodder & Stoughton, 1983, pp.127-8, himself quoting from Peter Marshall, *Mr Jones, Meet the Master*, Peter Davies Ltd (William Heinemann), 1954. Reprinted by permission of Reed Consumer Books.

The transforming Holy Spirit

Suggestions for prayer together

> As a deer longs for flowing streams,
> so my soul longs for you, O God.
> My soul thirsts for God,
> for the living God.
> When shall I come and behold the face of God?
>
> Psalm 42.1-2

> O God, you are my God, I seek you,
> my soul thirsts for you;
> my flesh faints for you,
> as in a dry and weary land where there is no water.
>
> Psalm 63.1

> Ho, everyone who thirsts,
> come to the waters;
>
> Isaiah 55.1

> Let anyone who is thirsty come to me, and let the one who believes in me drink.
> As the scripture has said, 'Out of the believer's heart shall flow rivers of living water.'
>
> John 7.37-8

> Let your living water flow over my soul.
> Let your Holy Spirit come and take control
> of every situation that has troubled my mind.
> All my cares and burdens onto you I roll.
>
> John Watson. Copyright © 1986 Ampelos Music. Administered by
> CopyCare, PO Box 77, Hailsham, BN27. Used by permission.

session
04]

The empowering Holy Spirit

Bible study and discussion: Luke 24.45-49; Acts 1.1-9

Welcome the group and invite anyone to share any observations, reflections or questions arising from last week's study.

Then read the two passages from the end of Luke's Gospel and the beginning of Acts.

The Holy Spirit is given to dwell within us and to transform us – but in these passages in particular the promise of the Holy Spirit is to empower Christian people for ministry.

The disciples have been given a difficult, if not impossible, commission to fulfil: to communicate the Christian gospel to the whole world. To execute that great commission, they need the empowering of the Spirit that was given at Pentecost.

Ask the group to brainstorm together for a few moments about why that empowering is needed. Write your answers on a large piece of paper.

Then read together the moment in the Scriptures when the empowering happened (Acts 2.1-3,12-13) and its results (Acts 2.41).

Buzz groups: Power for ministry

Think together around the following questions:

■ *Has anyone in the group any experience of being consciously empowered for ministry by the Holy Spirit?*

Some groups will need little prompting here and will be full of examples. Others may need more help in recognizing just where the Holy Spirit has been at work in their lives. Receiving strength beyond yourself to care for a disabled child or elderly relative can be just as much the empowering of the Spirit as preaching a sermon.

■ *What are the main areas of your life and ministry where you feel you need this empowering?*

It may help to make a list either for the whole group or for each person in the group. Again, don't forget to include home, work and community situations as well as church ones.

■ *How do you believe we seek this empowering together?*

It may be worth pointing out that it doesn't happen automatically. Jesus says 'Ask, and it will be given you' when he is talking about the Holy Spirit (in Luke 11.9). The disciples had to wait in the city until they were clothed with power from on high.

It's also important to make a distinction between the Spirit dwelling within a Christian person and those particular times when God anoints a particular person for a special ministry (as at Pentecost for the Apostles).

What kinds of thing should we expect to happen after this empowering? The basic answer, and the test, is 'good fruit' of whatever kind. That does not necessarily mean new Christians – it depends what the anointing is given for.

Input and discussion: The power and the gifts of the Spirit

The Early Church very soon realized that, although the Holy Spirit dwelt within every Christian, and the Holy Spirit was available to empower every Christian, the end result was never the same. We are not all empowered by the Spirit in the same way. Some are greatly used by God in one thing, others in another.

St Paul uses two great interwoven pictures to describe the Spirit's work in this way.

One is the picture of the Church as the Body of Christ. We are all parts of the body (the Latin word *membrum*, from which we get the word 'member', means a limb or part of the body). Like the different parts of the body, we are all very different, and we all fulfil a different function in the Body of Christ.

The most developed picture of the body in the New Testament is 1 Corinthians 12.12-30. You may want to look at the passage briefly together.

The second picture is of the Spirit as the bringer of gifts. He is, as one writer describes him, the Giving Gift. The Greek word for 'gifts' or 'graces' of God is *charismata* – the name from which we derive 'charismatic'. The charismatic tradition or movement in the Church has been the tradition that has rediscovered and re-emphasized the gifts or graces of the Holy Spirit, which are part of the Spirit's equipping or empowering for ministry.

As with the body picture, Paul emphasizes that there is one Spirit, but he gives different gifts to different people. You'll find the gifts picture (and descriptions of spiritual gifts) in 1 Corinthians 12.1-11 – where it flows into the picture of the Body; in Romans 12.3-8; and in Ephesians 4.7-13 – where the two images are intertwined.

Give people time, in twos and threes, to look briefly at the following Bible passages:

■   *1 Corinthians 12.1-11*

■   *Romans 12.3-8*

■   *Ephesians 4.7-13.*

Together make a list of all the different kinds of spiritual gift mentioned in the Scriptures.

In the discussion draw out the following points:

■   *The New Testament lists are not meant to be exhaustive or complete.*

■   *Some of the gifts are God blessing and making more fruitful what are natural human abilities (such as hospitality or administration).*

■   *Other gifts go beyond our natural abilities (such as prophecy or gifts of healing).*

■   *You may want to spend some time exploring and thinking through some of the less usual spiritual gifts, such as tongues, prophecy or healing.*

If you don't know much about these gifts yourself, the wisest thing may be to invite a guest to the group for this session who can share something about them at this point – or else, give an extra week to thinking about spiritual gifts. Your local Christian bookshop or your minister will be able to recommend other things you can listen to or read to deepen your knowledge of this area of the Christian life.

■   *The gifts of the Spirit were not given just to the first generation of Christians. They are for every generation of Christians and our Christian life and witness are greatly impoverished if, as a Church, we are not using and developing the different gifts.*

The doctrine that the gifts of the Spirit were only for the first century is called 'dispensationalism' and has been widely taught in some evangelical churches. The basic idea is that God gave his Church spiritual gifts until the Scriptures had been written down. From that time on, the Bible was sufficient.

There are two problems with this view: the first is that it cannot be supported from within the New Testament; the second is that God does still give these gifts to his Church and to his people, to our very great benefit and blessing.

Spend some time thinking about the different gifts of each member of the group – either as one discussion or in huddles of four or five people. Encourage the group to affirm the good things they see in one another – but to be thirsty for more.

End with a general question and answer time.

Bible study and discussion: The Holy Spirit as fire

This study is briefer than those in earlier sessions, because of the time taken on gifts of the Spirit.

Read again Acts 2.1-3.

Introduce this fourth great picture of the Spirit from this passage: tongues of fire came to rest on each one.

Ask one another: what is communicated to you by the picture of the Holy Spirit as fire?

People will probably be able to talk about pictures of empowering and warmth and fire within. They may not pick up the second strand of meaning in the fire picture: that of purification – the refiner's fire (see Malachi 3.2).

At the end of the discussion, emphasize that each of the last three pictures of the Spirit can be so different in terms of intensity:

- *A wind can be a gentle breath or a roaring hurricane.*

- *Water can be a drip or a trickle, or a raging river.*

- *Fire can be a gentle candle flame or a lightning bolt from heaven.*

Suggestions for prayer together: Renew us by your Spirit

There are no set prayers for this week. Each group will want to pray in its own way – either summing up the course so far (if this is the last session) or preparing for a session of worship and prayer for one another (see Epilogue).

Luke 11.9-13 would be a good reading to guide the prayer time.

People may also find it helpful to pray through and think about the great hymn 'Come down, O love divine' or the modern worship song 'Refiner's fire' during the prayer time and in the coming week.

Putting it into practice

Encourage the group to finish reading Acts and also to go on praying using the words from the hymns or songs.

Summary and example timings

	mins
Bible study and discussion: Luke 24.45-49; Acts 1.1-9	10
Buzz groups: Power for ministry	15
Input and discussion: The power and gifts of the Spirit	40
Bible study and discussion: The Holy Spirit as fire	10
Suggestions for prayer together	10
Putting it into practice	5

The empowering Holy Spirit **handout**

Bible study: Luke 24.45-49; Acts 1.1-9

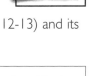

The promise of the Holy Spirit is to empower Christian people for ministry.

Why is that empowering needed?

Read the moment in the Scriptures when the empowering happened (Acts 2.1-3, 12-13) and its results (Acts 2.41).

> When the day of Pentecost had come, they were all together in one place. And suddenly from heaven there came a sound like the rush of a violent wind, and it filled the entire house where they were sitting. Divided tongues, as of fire, appeared among them, and a tongue rested on each of them . . . All were amazed and perplexed, saying to one another, 'What does this mean?' But others sneered and said, 'They are filled with new wine.'
>
> Acts 2.1-3,12-13

> So those who welcomed his message were baptized, and that day about three thousand persons were added.
>
> Acts 2.41

Power for ministry

Think around the following questions:

- *Have you any experience of being consciously empowered for ministry by the Holy Spirit?*

- *What are the main areas of your life and ministry where you feel you need this empowering?*

- *How do you believe we seek this empowering together?*

- *What kinds of thing should we expect to happen after this empowering?*

The power and the gifts of the Spirit

The early Church very soon realized that, although the Holy Spirit dwelt within every Christian, and the Holy Spirit was available to empower every Christian, the end result was never the same. We are not all empowered by the Spirit in the same way. Some are greatly used by God in one thing, others in another.

St Paul uses two great interwoven pictures to describe the Spirit's work in this way.

One is the picture of the Church as the Body of Christ. We are all parts of the body (the Latin word *membrum*, from which we get the word 'member', means a limb or part of the body). Like the different parts of the body, we are all very different, and we all fulfil a different function in the Body of Christ.

The second picture is of the Spirit as the bringer of gifts. He is, as one writer describes him, the Giving Gift.

As with the body picture, Paul emphasizes that there is one Spirit, but he gives different gifts to different people.

Look briefly at each Bible passage and make a list of all the different kinds of spiritual gift mentioned in the Scriptures.

_____

1 Corinthians 12.1-11

_____

Romans 12.3-8

_____

Ephesians 4.7-13

_____

- *The New Testament lists are not meant to be exhaustive or complete.*
- *Some of the gifts are God blessing and making more fruitful what are natural human abilities.*
- *Other gifts go beyond our natural abilities.*
- *The gifts of the Spirit were not given just to the first generation of Christians.*

Spend some time thinking about the different gifts of each member of the group.

The Holy Spirit as fire

Read again Acts 2.1-3.

What is communicated to you by the picture of the Holy Spirit as fire?

Putting it into practice

Go on using the prayers and songs from the course in preparation for the next session and finish reading Acts.

The empowering Holy Spirit

Suggestions for prayer: Renew us by your Spirit

Read Luke 11.9-13.

> So I say to you, Ask, and it will be given you; search, and you will find; knock, and the door will be opened for you. For everyone who asks receives, and everyone who searches finds, and for everyone who knocks, the door will be opened. Is there anyone among you who, if your child asks for a fish, will give a snake instead of a fish? Or if the child asks for an egg, will give a scorpion? If you then, who are evil, know how to give good gifts to your children, how much more will the heavenly Father give the Holy Spirit to those who ask him!

Come down, O love divine,
seek thou this soul of mine,
and visit it with thine own ardour glowing;
O comforter, draw near,
within my heart appear,
and kindle it, thy holy flame bestowing.

O let it freely burn,
till earthly passions turn
to dust and ashes in its heat consuming;
and let thy glorious light
shine ever on my sight,
and clothe me round, the while my path illuming.

Let holy charity
mine outward vesture be,
and lowliness become mine inner clothing:
true lowliness of heart,
which takes the humbler part,
and o'er its own shortcomings weeps with loathing.

And so the yearning strong,
with which the soul will long,
shall far outpass the power of human telling;
for none can guess its grace,
till he becomes the place
wherein the Holy Spirit makes his dwelling.

Bianco da Siena, trans. R. F. Littledale

Purify my heart,
let me be as gold and precious silver.
Purify my heart,
let me be as gold, pure gold.

Refiner's fire,
my heart's one desire
is to be holy,
set apart for you, Lord.
I choose to be holy,
set apart for you, my master,
ready to do your will.

Purify my heart,
cleanse me from within
and make me holy.
Purify my heart,
cleanse me from my sin,
deep within.

Epilogue

Ideas for a time of worship and prayer

These are ideas only. It's impossible to provide an outline that will suit every situation. When you think through how to focus, in a time of worship and prayer, what has been learned in the course, be open to the ideas of the group and to the leading of the Spirit.

- *Where will you hold the session?*

For some groups, it may be best to meet in your normal place. In others, meeting in church may be better.

- *Who will lead?*

Clearly the group leaders should be involved – but you may also want to include the ministers, priests or other leaders from your own church family.

- *What is a good structure?*

Here is one outline you could use. Ideally, different members of the group could be involved in preparing each part of the worship or prayers in advance.

1   A time of worship and praise – either sung or spoken

2   A time for sharing and reflection

The group leaders may sum up what has been learned through this part of *Emmaus*, using any Bible readings that have been particularly appropriate. There could be a time for any member of the group who wants to, to share something of what they have learned.

3   A time for prayer together

This could include an opportunity for confession; open prayer; or silence.

4   An opportunity for ministry

This should always be offered – and not compulsory. If you are meeting in a home, one idea would be to place a dining room chair in the middle of the room. Invite individuals who would like the whole group to pray for them with laying on of hands to come and sit on the chair (or stand, or kneel in the centre of the group). Two or three members of the group should then lay their hands on the person and ask God to fill them anew with the Holy Spirit. The rest of the group should pray quietly for the person. Pray in your own words – or in the words of the hymns and songs that have formed part of the course.

Allow as much time as you need to pray with each person.

If you are meeting in a church or chapel, indicate a place for people to come to kneel and receive prayer.

5   A time of praise and thanksgiving

End the session by focusing again on God, Father, Son and Holy Spirit in song or spoken praise.

Ideas for building on 'Come, Holy Spirit'

Ideas for going further are given in the supplementary handout that follows. You may like to duplicate this and ask the group to read it between meetings at the end of the course. When you next meet, go through the outline of what is suggested and allow the group to decide how it would like to take things forward.

If you do decide to include time and space for edification and using spiritual gifts within the meetings, be prepared for things to grow slowly and steadily rather than dramatically in the life of the group. Good fruit takes time to mature. Also take care not to allow times of sharing to become either too inward looking or too trivial in their subject matter. You will need the support of others in your church to reflect on what is happening and to guide the group forward.

Using 'Come, Holy Spirit' as a weekend conference

At a residential weekend

Residentials offer great opportunities for growing together in fellowship as well as for teaching. It's worth taking even a small group of a dozen away together. Christian hotels and conference centres can often fit a smaller group into their programme more easily than a full parish weekend. Planning a residential away, with different people undertaking different tasks, is a good way to move a group on.

Friday evening is usually not a good time for input on a residential because people have been working all day and have travelled to the venue. Keep the Friday night session fairly light and informal, with introductions to one another and to the material and some prayers.

On the Saturday morning, the teaching should cover the first two sessions of the course, with a coffee break between. Prayer and worship should be brief.

Saturday afternoon is best left free, with a third session of teaching and Bible study on Saturday evening, and the fourth on the first part of Sunday morning. The second part of Sunday morning can then be given over to worship and to ministry.

At a non-residential weekend

People need some time and space to carry on their own lives at home, as well as to take part in the course.

You could cover Session One on the Friday evening and Sessions Two and Three on the Saturday morning. Leave people free on Saturday afternoon and then cover Session Four either on Saturday evening or Sunday afternoon – perhaps with opportunity for ministry during or after a Sunday evening service.

As a day conference

This needs more concentrated input and may not be as valuable a learning experience. To fit the whole course into a day, teach the first two sessions on the Saturday morning and the last two on Saturday afternoon. The evening could then be given over to worship and ministry.

The empowering
Holy Spirit

Building on 'Come, Holy Spirit'

A four-week course on the Holy Spirit is able only to lay a foundation. If your group is to grow, particularly in using the gifts of the Holy Spirit, then you will need to give time and space to this part of Christian experience regularly as you meet together. The best way, in fact, to grow in the gifts the Spirit gives is in a small supportive group of Christian people.

In 1 Corinthians 14, Paul really encourages the Christians in Corinth to desire the gifts of the Spirit and to use them to build up the whole Church. He envisages a situation where the most common church meeting was a small group (see 1 Corinthians 16.19) in which every person's contribution can be recognized and used.

In verses 26 to 40, he envisages that each meeting of Christian people in a small group would include a time for different spiritual gifts to be used. This would not necessarily have been the whole meeting (which would have included more sustained teaching; or prayer; or communion). But it would have been an occasion when everyone's spiritual gift could be used and developed in a safe environment:

> When you come together, each one has a hymn, a lesson, a revelation, a tongue, or an interpretation. Let all things be done for building up. If anyone speaks in a tongue, let there be only two or at most three, and each in turn; and let one interpret. But if there is no one to interpret, let them be silent in church and speak to themselves and to God. Let two or three prophets speak, and let the others weigh what is said.
>
> 1 Corinthians 14.26-29

If this time of 'edification', or being open to spiritual gifts, is included in the prayer time of each meeting of the group, it will bring many benefits. The whole group will build each other up in faith through the gifts of the members. Each person will be encouraged to spend time in prayer before the group meets, in order to be able to bring a hymn, or a word of instruction or a prophecy. The group members themselves will come to 'own' the meeting instead of simply turning up and being served by the group leaders. People will begin to use their spiritual gift in a small group and grow to the degree that they are able to exercise a ministry beyond the group in their family, workplace or the wider Church.

Bibliography and further reading

Bibliography

John Blanchard, *Will the Real Jesus Please Stand Up*, Evangelical Press, 1989.

The Church of England Doctrine Commission, *The Mystery of Salvation*, Church House Publishing, 1995, now published in *Contemporary Doctrine Classics*, Church House Publishing, 2005.

Common Worship, Church House Publishing, 2000.

Steven Croft, *Growing New Christians*, CPAS/Marshall Pickering, 1993.

T. S. Eliot, Choruses from 'The Rock', *Collected Poems 1909–1962*, Faber & Faber, 1974.

Richard Foster, *Prayer*, Hodder & Stoughton, 1992.

Peter Marshall, *Mr Jones, Meet the Master*, Peter Davies Ltd (William Heinemann), 1954.

The New Revised Standard Version of the Bible, Division of Christian Education of the National Council of the Churches of Christ in the USA, 1989.

Henri Nouwen, *The Return of the Prodigal Son*, Darton, Longman & Todd, 1992.

Michael Perry (ed.), *The Dramatised Bible*, Marshall Pickering, 1988.

Yvonne Richmond, Nick Spencer, Rob Frost, Anne Richards, Mark Ireland, Steven Croft, *Evangelism in a Spiritual Age*, Church House Publishing, 2005.

N. T. Wright and M. J. Borg, *The Meaning of Jesus*, SPCK, 1999.

Further reading

Stephen Cottrell, *Praying through Life*, National Society/Church House Publishing, 1998.

Stephen Cottrell and Steven Croft, *Travelling Well: A Companion Guide to the Christian Faith*, National Society/Church House Publishing, 2000.

Steven Croft, *Missionary Journeys, Missionary Church: Acts 13 – 20*, National Society/Church House Publishing, 2001.

Steven Croft, *The Lord is Risen! Luke 24*, National Society/Church House Publishing, 2001.

Steven Croft, *Transforming Communities*, Darton, Longman & Todd, 2002.

The Doctrine Commission of the Church of England, *The Mystery of Salvation*, Church House Publishing, 1995, now available in *Contemporary Doctrine Classics*, Church House Publishing, 2005.

John Finney, *Emerging Evangelism*, Darton, Longman & Todd, 2004.

Bill and Lynne Hybels, *Rediscovering Church*, Zondervan, 1995.

C. S. Lewis, *Mere Christianity*, Collins Fontana Books, 1952.

Charles R. Swindoll, *Improving your Serve*, Hodder & Stoughton, 1983.

William Temple, *Readings in St John's Gospel*, Macmillan, 1947.

Robert Warren, *An Affair of the Heart*, Highland, 1994.

Robert Warren and Sue Mayfield, *Life Attitudes*, Church House Publishing, 2004.

A Wee Worship Book, Wild Goose Worship Group, 1989.

John Young, *Teach Yourself Christianity*, Hodder & Stoughton, 2003.

The authors

Stephen Cottrell is the Bishop of Reading. Prior to this he was Canon Pastor at Peterborough Cathedral and also worked for Springboard, the Archbishops' initiative for evangelism. His books include *Catholic Evangelism, Praying Through Life, I Thirst*, the Archbishop of Canterbury's Lent book for 2004, and, with Steven Croft, *Travelling Well: A companion guide to the Christian life*.

Steven Croft is Archbishops' Missioner and Team Leader of Fresh Expressions. He was previously Warden of Cranmer Hall in Durham and before that was a vicar in Halifax and mission consultant in Wakefield Diocese. He is the author of the handbooks *Growing New Christians* and *Making New Disciples*, and his work has pioneered understanding of the relationship between evangelism and nurture. His recent work includes *Ministry in Three Dimensions: Ordination and Leadership in the Local Church, Transforming Communities* and *Evangelism in a Spiritual Age*.

John Finney is the retired Bishop of Pontefract and former Decade of Evangelism Officer for the Church of England. His research report *Finding Faith Today* has been instrumental in helping the Church understand how people become Christians. He was also involved in the writing of *On the Way – Towards an Integrated Approach to Christian Initiation* for General Synod and is the author of several books on evangelism and renewal.

Felicity Lawson has been Dean of Ministry and Director of Ordinands in the Diocese of Wakefield. Together with John Finney she wrote *Saints Alive!*, a nurture course helping Christians towards a deeper understanding of the life in the Spirit. She has recently returned to parish ministry as Vicar of Gildersome, near Leeds.

Robert Warren was Team Rector of one of the largest and fastest growing churches in England, St Thomas, Crookes. In 1993 he succeeded John Finney as the Church of England's National Officer for Evangelism. In 1998 he became a full-time member of the Springboard team. He is the author of a number of books, including *Building Missionary Congregations*, which points to the task of helping people on the journey of faith as one of the key tasks for the Church in the twenty-first century, and *The Healthy Churches' Handbook*.

Although all five authors are Anglicans, the *Emmaus* material can be used by any denomination and has been produced with this in mind.

Using the CD-ROM

Running the CD-ROM

Windows PC users:
The CD-ROM should start automatically. If you need to start the application manually, click on *Start* and select *Run*, then type **d:\knowing.exe** (where **d** is the letter of your CD-ROM drive) and click on OK. The menu that appears gives you access to all the resources on the CD. No software is installed on to your computer.

Mac users:
Use the Finder to locate the resources in the folders described below. The menu application will not work on a Mac, but you will still be able to access the resources.

Viruses
We have checked the CD-ROM for viruses throughout its creation. However, you are advised to run your own virus-checking software over the CD-ROM before using it. Church House Publishing and The Archbishops' Council accept no responsibility for damage or loss of data on your systems, however caused.

Copyright
The material on the CD-ROM is copyright © The Archbishops' Council 2005, unless otherwise specified. All industry trademarks are acknowledged. You are free to use this material within your own church or group, but the material must not be further distributed in any form without written permission from Church House Publishing. When using images or resources from the CD-ROM please include the appropriate copyright notice.

Handouts
The written resources require *Adobe Acrobat Reader* for display and printing. If *Acrobat Reader* is already installed on your computer, it will be loaded automatically whenever required. If you do not have it, you can install *Acrobat Reader* from the program within the **acrobat** folder on the CD, or by downloading the Reader from www.adobe.com. Please note that Acrobat files cannot be edited.

Error messages
You may receive the error message, 'There is no application associated with the given file name extension.' If you are trying to read one of the handouts, you should install the *Adobe Acrobat Reader* and try again. If you are opening one of the image files, your system does not have any software registered for use with JPEG or TIFF files. Install the free copy of IrfanView and during its installation make sure you associate .TIF and .JPG extensions with IrfanView.

PowerPoint presentation
The CD-ROM contains presentations on *Emmaus* using Microsoft's PowerPoint. This will enable you to present the key facts about the course to groups within your church.

If you have PowerPoint 97 or later installed on your computer, you can use it to run the presentation directly from the CD. The presentations are in named folders within the **ppt** folder on the CD. If you do not have PowerPoint, install the free viewer **PPView97.exe** from the **ppt** folder itself.

If the text in the presentation is poorly displayed, use the version of the presentation called pngsetup.exe. This will copy the presentation to your PC, complete with embedded fonts.

Links
The links to web sites require an active Internet connection. Please ensure you can browse the web before selecting an external web site. We accept no responsibility for the content of sites not produced by Church House Publishing.

Further help
If you experience problems with the CD, please visit the *Emmaus* web site at www.e-mmaus.org.uk We will post further help or support issues on this site.

Emmaus: The Way of Faith

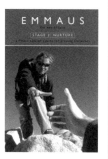

If you have enjoyed using *Knowing God*, you may be interested in the other *Emmaus: The Way of Faith* material.

Resources for leaders

Emmaus: The Way of Faith Introduction (2nd edition)
£4.95   0 7151 4963 6
Essential background to both the theology and practice of *Emmaus* and includes material on how to run the course in your own church.

Leading an Emmaus Group (2nd edition)
£5.95   0 7151 4025 6
Straightforward and direct guide to leading both Nurture and Growth groups. It lays a biblical framework for group leadership, using Jesus as the example and model.

Contact (2nd edition)
£5.95   0 7151 4995 4
Explores ways that your church can be involved in evangelism and outreach and make contact with those outside the Church.

Emmaus courses

Nurture (2nd edition)
£22.50   0 7151 4994 6 *Includes CD-ROM*
A 15-session course covering the basics of Christian life and faith.

Growth: Growing as a Christian (2nd edition)
£22.50   0 7151 4014 0 *Includes CD-ROM*
Five short courses for growing Christians: Growing in Prayer; Growing in the Scriptures; Being Church; Growing in Worship; and Life, Death and Christian Hope.

Growth: Christian Lifestyle (2nd edition)
£22.50   0 7151 4006 X *Includes CD-ROM*
Four short courses for growing Christians: Living Images; Overcoming Evil; Personal Identity; and Called into Life.

Youth Emmaus
£19.95   0 7151 4988 1 *Includes CD-ROM*
Aimed specifically at young people aged 11–16, *Youth Emmaus* tackles the basics of the Christian faith. Ideal for teenage confirmation candidates.

Downloadable samples available at www.e-mmaus.org.uk

Emmaus Bible Resources – Ideal for small groups!

Finding a middle ground between daily Bible notes and weighty commentaries, the series adopts the *Emmaus* approach of combining sound theology and good educational practice with a commitment to equip the whole Church for mission.

Each book contains leader's guidelines, short prayers or meditations, a commentary, discussion questions and practical 'follow-on' activities.

The Lord is Risen!
Luke 24
Steven Croft   £7.95   0 7151 4971 7
The Lord is Risen! takes us on a journey through Luke that strengthens, challenges, deepens and renews our Christian discipleship. An ideal 'Easter' book.

Missionary Journeys, Missionary Church
Acts 13-20
Steven Croft   £7.95   0 7151 4972 5
Throughout Christian history, men and women have returned to the book of Acts to find their faith and ministry renewed and rekindled.

A Rebellious Prophet
Jonah
Joy Tetley   £7.95   0 7151 4986 5
As Christians, we are not all called to be prophets. But we are all called to respond to God's prompting. This study of the book of Jonah challenges us to do just that.

Christ our Life
Colossians
David Day   £7.95   0 7151 4987 3
Colossians was written to a church set in a culture dominated by powerful forces and alternative spiritualities. David Day's perceptive book encourages us to consider how to give Christ his rightful place in every area of our lives, both personal and corporate.

Resources for course group members

Travelling Well
A Companion Guide to the Christian Life
Stephen Cottrell and Steven Croft
£7.95   0 7151 4935 0
In a warm, accessible style, *Travelling Well* encourages new Christians in their journey of faith. Offers practical advice and wisdom on prayer, reading the Bible, worship and relating faith to daily life. Ideal for adult Christians who are beginning the journey of faith.

Praying Through Life (2nd edition)
How to pray in the home, at work and in the family
Stephen Cottrell
£7.95   0 7151 4010 8
Prayer is a challenge for most Christians. This honest and refreshing book explores ways to start, renew and expand our prayer life, whether by ourselves or with others. It helps us discover how natural prayer can be, even when we least feel like it.

FOOTNOTE
If you would like to receive regular updates please join the *Emmaus* database.

Send your details to Emmaus, Church House Publishing, Great Smith Street, London, SW1P 3NZ, email emmaus@c-of-e.org.uk or call 020 7898 1451.

www.e-mmaus.org.uk